Title: *The Art of Winning: Strategies from Sports, Business, and Life*
Subtitle: *Master the Mindset and Skills of Champions to Achieve Success*

James Fletcher

Table of Contents

Introduction: The Art of Winning

Chapter 1: Think Like a Winner

Chapter 2: Thriving Under Pressure

Chapter 3: Strategic Thinking – Winning Before the Battle Begins

Chapter 4: Communication Mastery – The Language of Winning

Chapter 5: Time Management – Winning the Race Against the Clock

Chapter 6: The Power of Habits – Daily Routines That Drive Success

Chapter 7: Resilience – Bouncing Back Stronger Than Ever

Chapter 8: Teamwork – The Power of Collaboration

Chapter 9: Leadership – Inspiring Others to Follow

Chapter 10: Confidence – The Key to Self-Belief and Success

Chapter 11: Focus – The Power of Eliminating Distractions

Chapter 12: Balance – The Key to Sustained Success and Well-Being

Chapter 13: Motivation – Staying Driven for the Long Haul

Chapter 14: Gratitude – The Transformative Power of Appreciation

Chapter 15: Legacy – Creating a Lasting Impact

Chapter 16: Lifelong Learning – The Journey of Continuous Growth

Chapter 17: Mindfulness – Staying Grounded in a Busy World

Chapter 18: Generosity – Giving Back to Amplify Success

Chapter 19: Courage – Taking Risks and Seizing Opportunities

Chapter 20: Optimism – Cultivating a Positive Mindset for Success

Chapter 21: Decision-Making – Taking Bold, Decisive Actions

Chapter 22: Building Relationships – The Foundation of Long-Term Success

Chapter 23: Resilience – Turning Setbacks into Stepping Stones

Chapter 24: Discipline – Staying Consistent on the Path to Success

Chapter 25: Creativity and Innovation – Staying Ahead in a Competitive World

Chapter 26: Leadership – Inspiring and Empowering Others

Chapter 27: Balance and Fulfilment – Achieving Harmony Amid Ambition

James Fletcher

Introduction: The Art of Winning

What does it mean to win?

For some, winning is lifting a championship trophy or sealing a lucrative business deal. For others, it's overcoming adversity, achieving personal goals, or simply finding happiness in the everyday hustle of life. Winning is deeply personal, yet universally desired. It's the thrill of reaching for something extraordinary and seeing it through to the finish line.

But winning isn't just about the big moments. It's a mindset—a way of approaching life with purpose, determination, and a refusal to settle for less than your best. Whether you're an athlete aiming for glory, an entrepreneur chasing innovation, or a parent striving to create a better future for your family, the principles of winning are the same. And the best part? They can be learned.

I wasn't born with a champion's mindset. Like most people, I've stumbled, faced setbacks, and doubted my ability to succeed. I've felt the sting of failure and the frustration of being stuck.

But through observing great achievers, studying what makes them tick, and applying those lessons to my own life, I discovered that winning isn't about talent alone—it's about preparation, strategy, and the willingness to push through when things get tough.

This book is a roadmap for winning, not just in the conventional sense, but in all areas of life. We'll explore the mental toughness of Olympic athletes, the game-changing strategies of successful CEOs, and the quiet, everyday victories that pave the way for lasting fulfilment. Along the way, I'll share stories from the worlds of sports, business, and life, weaving them with actionable insights you can apply immediately.

You don't need to be born a winner to become one. By adopting the habits, mindset, and strategies of champions, you can achieve more than you ever thought possible. This is your guide to unlocking that potential and winning in every sense of the word.

The journey begins here. Let's get to work.

Chapter 1: Think Like a Winner

Winning doesn't begin on the pitch, in the boardroom, or at the starting line. It begins in the mind. The way you think—your attitudes, beliefs, and mental habits—determines the heights you'll reach. Champions aren't born; they're built, often from the inside out. If you want to achieve greatness in any area of life, the first step is learning to think like a winner.

The Power of Belief

In 1954, Roger Bannister shattered a barrier that had stood for centuries: the four-minute mile. Before Bannister's achievement, scientists and coaches claimed it was physiologically impossible. But as soon as Bannister broke the barrier, others quickly followed. What changed? The physical capabilities of the human body hadn't evolved overnight. Instead, Bannister's triumph rewired the collective belief of athletes worldwide. He showed them what was possible.

Belief is the foundation of every achievement. Whether you want to build a thriving business, become a top athlete, or lead a fulfilling life, belief fuels the actions that make it possible.

Belief doesn't mean ignoring reality or wishing away challenges; it's about seeing potential where others see obstacles and daring to act on that potential.

Ask yourself: Do you truly believe you can achieve your goals? If not, what's holding you back? Identifying and addressing those mental barriers is the first step toward victory.

The Winner's Mindset: Five Core Principles

1. **Failure is Feedback, Not Final**
   Thomas Edison famously said, "I have not failed. I've just found 10,000 ways that won't work." Winners don't see failure as an endpoint but as a step on the journey to success. Every missed shot, lost deal, or failed project is an opportunity to learn. Michael Jordan, one of the greatest basketball players of all time, missed over 9,000 shots in his career, lost almost 300 games, and failed to make the game-winning shot 26 times. Yet, he credits those failures as the reason for his success.

   Challenge yourself to reframe failure. Instead of asking, "Why me?" ask, "What can I learn?" Each setback is a stepping stone, not a roadblock.

2. **Focus on What You Can Control**
Life throws curveballs: unfair decisions, unexpected setbacks, and tough breaks. Winners focus on the controllable. In sports, this might mean training harder or adapting strategy. In business, it's staying prepared and maintaining composure under pressure.

Worrying about external factors drains energy and leads to frustration. Instead, channel that energy into areas where you have influence—your effort, attitude, and preparation. By controlling your response to challenges, you regain power over the situation.

3. **See Challenges as Opportunities**
Every great success story is born from adversity. When Serena Williams faced career-threatening injuries and personal criticism, she used those moments as fuel to return stronger, eventually becoming one of the greatest athletes of all time. Challenges can either break you or build you—the choice is yours.

Winners adopt a growth mindset, viewing every obstacle as an opportunity to improve. Instead of saying, "Why is this happening to me?" ask, "How can this make me better?"

4. **The Power of Persistence**
   Most people give up too soon. Winners understand that success often requires outlasting the competition. Think of J.K. Rowling, whose manuscript for *Harry Potter* was rejected by 12 publishers before being accepted. Her persistence paid off, and she became one of the best-selling authors in history.

   Persistence doesn't mean blindly repeating the same actions. It means learning, adapting, and continuing to move forward, even when progress feels slow.

5. **Stay Focused on the Bigger Picture**
   It's easy to get bogged down in minor setbacks or short-term distractions. Winners keep their eyes on the prize. They understand that short-term discomfort is often necessary for long-term gain.

Visualisation is a powerful tool to maintain focus. Imagine yourself achieving your goal in vivid detail—what it looks, feels, and sounds like. This mental rehearsal not only motivates you but also programs your brain to seek out opportunities and solutions.

Rewriting Your Inner Narrative

Everyone of us has an inner voice. For some, it's a constant critic, pointing out flaws and amplifying fears. For others, it's a coach, encouraging and guiding them toward success. To think like a winner, you must train your inner voice to work for you, not against you.

Start by identifying negative self-talk. Do you tell yourself, "I'm not good enough" or "I'll never succeed"? Replace these thoughts with empowering affirmations:

- "I'm capable of learning and growing."
- "I've overcome challenges before, and I can do it again."
- "Every step I take brings me closer to my goals."

Consistency is key. Over time, these affirmations will become second nature, strengthening your confidence and resilience.

The Science of Visualisation

Winners don't just dream about success—they *see* it. Visualisation is a technique used by elite athletes, entrepreneurs, and performers to prepare for success. Studies show that mentally rehearsing success activates the same neural pathways as physical practice, making it a powerful tool for performance.

How to visualise effectively:

1. **Be Specific**: Don't just imagine "winning." Picture the details—how you'll feel, what you'll do, and who will be there.
2. **Engage Your Senses**: Include sights, sounds, and emotions in your visualisation.
3. **Practice Regularly**: Spend a few minutes each day visualising your goals.

Action Steps: Train Your Mind Like a Champion

1. **Morning Affirmations**: Start each day by repeating three positive affirmations about yourself or your goals.
2. **Gratitude Journal**: Write down three things you're grateful for each evening. Gratitude shifts your focus from what's missing to what's possible.

3. **Create a Vision Board**: Collect images, quotes, and symbols that represent your goals. Display them somewhere visible to keep your focus sharp.
4. **Meditation and Mindfulness**: Spend 5–10 minutes each day quieting your mind and focusing on your breathing. This improves clarity and reduces stress.

Conclusion: It All Begins in the Mind

Thinking like a winner isn't about ignoring reality or pretending life is easy. It's about choosing to see possibilities where others see problems. It's about training your mind to stay focused, resilient, and optimistic, even in the face of challenges.

As you move through this book, you'll discover more tools and strategies to help you win in every area of life. But remember it all starts here, with the decision to believe in yourself and commit to the journey.

In the next chapter, we'll explore how winners thrive under pressure and turn adversity into opportunity. But for now, ask yourself: What's one thing I can do today to start thinking like a winner?

Chapter 2: Thriving Under Pressure

Pressure is inevitable. Whether you're facing a critical deadline at work, stepping onto the field for a championship game, or navigating personal challenges, moments of high stress are part of life. The difference between winners and everyone else isn't the absence of pressure—it's their ability to thrive in it.

Winners don't crumble under the weight of expectations; they rise to meet them. They see pressure not as a threat, but as an opportunity to grow, adapt, and perform at their best. In this chapter, we'll explore how to develop that same resilience and use pressure as a catalyst for success.

Why Pressure Is a Privilege

Billie Jean King, one of the greatest tennis players of all time, famously said, "Pressure is a privilege." It means you're in a position where your actions matter, where the stakes are high enough to create change. Pressure signals that you're stepping into an arena that challenges your skills and pushes you to your limits.

Instead of dreading high-pressure situations, winners embrace them as opportunities to test their abilities. They know that the moments when the stakes are highest are often the ones that define their careers and lives.

Ask yourself: Do you see pressure as something to fear or something to welcome? Reframing your mindset around pressure is the first step toward thriving in it.

The Science of Pressure and Performance

The relationship between pressure and performance is often illustrated by the Yerkes-Dodson Law, which shows that moderate levels of pressure improve performance, but too much can lead to a breakdown. The key is to find your "sweet spot," where the pressure motivates and sharpens you without becoming overwhelming.

Understanding your own stress threshold can help you manage high-pressure situations more effectively. What might push one person to their limit could energise another. Self-awareness is critical to recognising when to step back and recalibrate.

Techniques to Stay Calm and Focused Under Pressure

1. **Control Your Breath**
   One of the quickest ways to calm your mind is through controlled breathing. Deep, rhythmic breathing activates the parasympathetic nervous system, reducing stress and restoring focus.
   - Try this: Inhale deeply for four seconds, hold your breath for four seconds, and exhale slowly for six seconds. Repeat this cycle five times to regain clarity in high-pressure moments.

2. **Break It Down**
   Pressure often feels overwhelming because we focus on the enormity of the task ahead. Winners break big challenges into smaller, manageable steps. Instead of thinking about winning the whole match, they focus on winning the next point.

   Ask yourself: What's the next best action I can take? Focusing on immediate, achievable goals reduces anxiety and builds momentum.

3. **Prepare for Pressure**
   Champions don't wait for the big moment to practice staying calm—they prepare for it. By simulating pressure in training, they're ready when it counts. For example, Olympic athletes often rehearse their routines with intentional distractions or tight time constraints to mimic competition-day stress.

   How can you prepare for pressure in your own life? Practice difficult conversations, rehearse presentations, or simulate high-stakes scenarios to build your resilience.

4. **Visualise Success**
   Visualisation isn't just about imagining the end goal; it's also about mentally rehearsing how you'll handle pressure along the way. Picture yourself staying composed and confident in the face of challenges.

   Studies show that athletes who visualise both their successes and the obstacles they'll face perform better than those who only focus on the positives. Be realistic in your visualisations, and you'll feel more prepared when the pressure hits.

5. **Develop a Pre-Performance Routine**
   Many winners have rituals that help them stay grounded before high-pressure moments. Whether it's listening to a specific playlist, repeating a mantra, or reviewing a checklist, routines create a sense of control and reduce anxiety.

   Create a personal routine that calms your nerves and puts you in the zone.

Turning Pressure into Fuel

Winners don't just survive pressure—they use it to fuel their performance. Here's how:

1. **Shift Your Perspective**
   Instead of saying, "I have to do this," reframe it as "I get to do this." Recognise that the pressure you're feeling is a sign of growth and opportunity.
2. **Channel Your Adrenaline**
   Pressure often triggers the body's fight-or-flight response, releasing adrenaline. Instead of letting this energy overwhelm you, channel it into focused effort. Many performers describe feeling "alive" under pressure because they've learned to harness this energy for peak performance.

3. **Learn from the Best**
   Study how top performers handle pressure. Take Serena Williams, for example. She thrives in the final moments of a match because she's trained her mind to see those moments as exciting rather than intimidating.

   Find role models in your field and learn how they stay composed under stress.

Case Study: Tom Brady and the Super Bowl Comeback

One of the most iconic examples of thriving under pressure is Tom Brady's performance in Super Bowl LI. The New England Patriots were down 28–3 in the third quarter, a deficit so large that most teams would have mentally checked out. But Brady stayed calm, focused on one play at a time, and led his team to a historic overtime victory.

How did he do it? By blocking out the noise, trusting his preparation, and staying present in the moment. Brady's ability to perform under extreme pressure cemented his legacy as one of the greatest quarterbacks of all time.

Action Steps: Build Your Resilience Under Pressure

1. **Practice Under Stress**
   Create situations in your daily life where you intentionally put yourself under mild stress. For example, give yourself a shorter deadline for a task or practice a presentation in front of friends. The more you expose yourself to controlled pressure, the more comfortable you'll be when it's real.
2. **Use Positive Self-Talk**
   Replace negative thoughts like "I can't handle this" with empowering statements like "I've prepared for this moment" or "I thrive under pressure."
3. **Celebrate Small Wins**
   After every high-pressure situation, reflect on what went well and what you learned. Celebrate your ability to navigate stress successfully.

Conclusion: Your Greatest Growth Comes Under Pressure

Pressure is often viewed as the enemy of success, but it's actually one of its greatest allies. The moments that challenge you the most are the ones that shape your character, sharpen your skills, and prepare you for even greater victories.

Thriving under pressure isn't about eliminating stress—it's about managing it effectively and using it as a tool for growth. As you face high-stakes situations in your own life, remember pressure is a privilege, and how you respond to it is what sets you apart.

In the next chapter, we'll dive into strategic thinking and how winners use foresight and planning to outmanoeuvre their competition. But for now, ask yourself: What's one high-pressure situation you've faced recently, and how can you use it to grow?

Let's rise to the challenge.

Chapter 3: Strategic Thinking – Winning Before the Battle Begins

Winners don't rely on luck to succeed. They prepare, analyse, and plan. Strategic thinking isn't just about making decisions in the moment—it's about positioning yourself for success long before the stakes are high. Whether you're leading a team, competing on the field, or managing your personal goals, a winning strategy makes all the difference.

In this chapter, we'll explore how winners use foresight, adaptability, and planning to stay ahead of the competition. From sports icons to business titans, the ability to think strategically is a hallmark of success.

The Power of Planning

"Victorious warriors win first and then go to war, while defeated warriors go to war first and then seek to win." – Sun Tzu, *The Art of War*

Great achievements don't happen by accident. Behind every major success is a plan—a roadmap that guides decisions, mitigates risks, and ensures progress. Winners approach challenges with clarity and intention.

Consider Lionel Messi's precision on the football field. His brilliance isn't just instinct; it's a product of preparation. He studies opponents, anticipates their moves, and positions himself to exploit opportunities.

Strategic thinking is about more than just having a plan; it's about creating a plan that accounts for variables, anticipates obstacles, and allows for flexibility when things don't go as expected.

The Principles of Strategic Thinking

1. **Define Your Goal Clearly**
   Winners know what they're aiming for. Whether it's winning a championship, closing a deal, or achieving a personal milestone, clarity of purpose is essential. Without a clear goal, even the best strategies will falter.
   - Ask yourself: What does success look like? Break your goal down into measurable outcomes and timelines.

2. **Understand Your Environment**
   Strategic thinking requires an awareness of your surroundings. This means analysing the competition, recognising opportunities, and identifying potential obstacles.
   - In business, this could mean conducting a SWOT analysis (Strengths, Weaknesses, Opportunities, Threats).
   - In sports, it might mean studying the tactics of opposing teams or reviewing past performance.

   Winners don't operate in isolation; they constantly evaluate the landscape to stay ahead.

3. **Think Two Steps Ahead**
   Winners anticipate not only the immediate impact of their decisions but also the long-term consequences. Like chess players, they consider the ripple effects of every move.
   - Before making a decision, ask: "If I do this, what happens next? And then what?" Strategic thinkers play out scenarios in their minds to prepare for all possibilities.

4. **Be Flexible and Adaptable**
   No plan survives contact with reality. Unexpected challenges are inevitable, and winners know how to pivot without losing sight of their goals. Adaptability isn't about abandoning your strategy; it's about adjusting it to fit the circumstances.

   Think of Serena Williams: when her opponent disrupts her rhythm, she adjusts her game plan mid-match, using her versatility to regain control.

5. **Leverage Your Strengths**
   Winners play to their strengths and minimise their weaknesses. They focus on what they do best, rather than trying to excel at everything.
   - Ask yourself: What are my unique skills or resources? How can I use them to gain an advantage?

Case Study: Elon Musk and Strategic Thinking

Elon Musk's rise to global success is a masterclass in strategic thinking. From revolutionising electric vehicles with Tesla to redefining space exploration with SpaceX, Musk has consistently stayed ahead of the curve by anticipating industry trends and positioning himself to lead.

For example, when founding Tesla, Musk didn't start with mass-market electric cars. Instead, he launched with the high-end Roadster to prove the viability of electric vehicles. Once Tesla gained credibility, he used that momentum to develop more affordable models like the Model S and Model 3.

This phased approach—starting small, proving the concept, and scaling up—demonstrates the power of strategic thinking.

Developing Your Strategic Thinking Skills

1. **Start with the End in Mind**
   Begin every project, challenge, or goal by envisioning the desired outcome. Write down your vision and reverse-engineer the steps needed to achieve it.

- For example: If your goal is to lose weight, break it into actionable steps like meal planning, exercise routines, and progress tracking.

2. **Analyse the Competition**
Whether in sports, business, or personal goals, understanding your competition is critical. Ask yourself:
    - What are their strengths and weaknesses?
    - How can I differentiate myself?

In sports, this might mean reviewing game footage. In business, it could involve market research.

3. **Identify Key Milestones**
Break your goal into smaller, measurable checkpoints. This makes large goals feel manageable and allows you to track progress.
    - For example: If your goal is to save £10,000, set monthly savings targets and adjust your strategy as needed.

4. **Plan for Contingencies**
   A good strategy accounts for uncertainty. Create a backup plan for potential obstacles. This might mean saving extra funds for unexpected expenses or having an alternative approach ready if your first attempt fails.
5. **Seek Outside Perspectives**
   Strategic thinkers don't operate in silos. They seek input from mentors, peers, or experts to refine their plans.

Action Steps: Apply Strategic Thinking to Your Life

1. **Conduct a Personal SWOT Analysis**
   - **Strengths:** What are you naturally good at?
   - **Weaknesses:** What holds you back?
   - **Opportunities:** What advantages can you leverage?
   - **Threats:** What challenges or risks might you face?

   Write these down and use them to inform your strategy.

2. **Practice Scenario Planning**
   For any major decision, play out at least three possible scenarios: best-case, worst-case, and most likely. This prepares you for whatever comes your way.
3. **Track Your Progress**
   Use tools like journals, spreadsheets, or apps to monitor your progress toward goals. Regularly review and adjust your strategy based on what's working and what isn't.
4. **Adopt a Long-Term View**
   Think beyond immediate results. Ask: How will this decision impact me in a year, five years, or ten years? Strategic thinkers prioritise sustainable success over short-term gains.

Conclusion: Strategy Is the Foundation of Victory

Strategic thinking isn't a skill reserved for CEOs, elite athletes, or military leaders. It's a mindset that anyone can develop and apply to their life. When you approach challenges with a clear plan, anticipate obstacles, and adapt as needed, you set yourself up for success.

In the next chapter, we'll explore the importance of communication—how winners build trust, inspire teams, and navigate difficult conversations with confidence. But before you move on, ask yourself: What's one area of your life where you can apply strategic thinking today?

The battle is won before it begins—if you're prepared.

Chapter 4: Communication Mastery – The Language of Winning

If strategy lays the groundwork for success, communication is the bridge that connects plans to execution. Whether you're leading a team, negotiating a deal, or simply building relationships, the ability to communicate effectively is a game-changer. Winners know that words are powerful tools—they can inspire, motivate, and influence those around them.

In the UK, where effective communication often balances politeness with precision, mastering the art of clear, impactful dialogue is even more crucial. From the football pitch to the boardroom, the best leaders and performers are also excellent communicators. In this chapter, we'll explore how winners use their words to connect, inspire, and achieve their goals.

The Power of Communication

Great communicators don't just speak; they connect. Consider Gareth Southgate, manager of the England football team. Southgate is renowned not only for his tactical acumen but also for his ability to inspire players and the nation alike.

His calm, empathetic communication style brought the team together, fostering trust and unity during high-pressure moments.

Effective communication is about more than just getting your message across—it's about understanding your audience, listening actively, and adapting your style to suit the situation.

Key Principles of Effective Communication

1. **Clarity is Key**
   Winners don't hide behind jargon or overly complex language. They speak clearly and directly, ensuring their message is understood. In the UK, where indirect communication is common, clarity doesn't mean being blunt—it means being concise and considerate.
   - Instead of saying, "We might want to consider possibly adjusting our approach," say, "Let's adjust our approach to achieve better results."
2. **Listen More Than You Speak**
   Active listening is the foundation of great communication. It shows respect, builds trust, and ensures you truly understand others' perspectives. Winners listen not just to respond but to learn.

- In meetings or conversations, summarise what you've heard to confirm understanding: "So, you're suggesting we focus on X—is that right?"

3. **Adapt to Your Audience**
Effective communicators tailor their style to suit their audience. Whether you're addressing a room full of executives, speaking to teammates, or explaining something to a child, adjust your tone, vocabulary, and delivery to make your message resonate.
    - In the UK workplace, this might mean balancing professionalism with approachability.

4. **Non-Verbal Cues Matter**
Communication isn't just about words—it's also about body language, tone, and eye contact. Winners ensure their non-verbal cues align with their message.
    - Maintain good posture, make eye contact, and use a confident but warm tone to build trust and credibility.

5. **Empathy Builds Connections**
   Understanding others' feelings and perspectives makes you a better communicator. In the UK, where politeness and consideration are cultural staples, empathy is especially important.
   - Phrases like, "I see where you're coming from" or "That must have been challenging" go a long way in creating rapport.

Case Study: Sir Alex Ferguson and Leadership Communication

One of the UK's most iconic leaders, Sir Alex Ferguson, exemplifies the power of communication. During his 26 years as Manchester United manager, Ferguson was a master at motivating players, managing egos, and inspiring excellence.

Ferguson tailored his communication style to fit each situation. He knew when to give a fiery half-time speech to ignite passion and when to offer a quiet word of encouragement to boost confidence. His ability to connect with players on a personal level created a winning culture at Old Trafford.

The lesson: Great communication isn't one-size-fits-all. It's about understanding the moment and choosing the right words, tone, and approach.

The Art of Persuasion

Communication mastery isn't just about conveying information—it's about influencing and persuading. Winners know how to present their ideas in a way that inspires action.

1. **Build Trust First**
   People are more likely to be persuaded by someone they trust. Be honest, transparent, and consistent in your words and actions.
2. **Use Stories to Connect**
   Stories are powerful because they evoke emotion and make ideas memorable. Instead of presenting dry facts, weave them into a narrative that resonates with your audience.
   - For example, if you're pitching an idea at work, share a story about how a similar approach succeeded in the past.

3. **Highlight Benefits, Not Just Features**
   When persuading, focus on what's in it for your audience. Instead of saying, "This plan will reduce costs by 10%," say, "This plan will free up budget for more exciting opportunities."

Handling Difficult Conversations

Not all communication is easy. Winners excel at navigating difficult conversations, whether it's delivering criticism, resolving conflicts, or negotiating tough deals.

1. **Prepare Ahead of Time**
   Before a difficult conversation, clarify your goals and anticipate potential objections. This ensures you stay focused and composed.
2. **Start with Empathy**
   Acknowledge the other person's perspective before presenting your own. In the UK, where politeness is highly valued, starting with empathy sets a positive tone.
   - For example: "I understand this is a challenging situation for you. Here's what I think we can do to address it."

3. **Focus on Solutions**
   Instead of dwelling on problems, steer the conversation toward actionable solutions. This keeps the tone constructive and forward-looking.
4. **Stay Calm and Professional**
   In tense situations, emotions can run high. Winners maintain composure and focus on the issue, not the person.

Practical Steps to Master Communication

1. **Practice Active Listening Daily**
   Make a conscious effort to listen more during conversations. Ask follow-up questions to show genuine interest and understanding.
2. **Seek Feedback**
   Ask colleagues, friends, or mentors for feedback on your communication style. What are your strengths? What could you improve?
3. **Record and Review Yourself**
   If you're preparing for a presentation or important meeting, record yourself speaking. Reviewing your delivery helps you identify areas for improvement, such as tone, pacing, or clarity.

4. **Read and Write Regularly**
   Strong communicators are often avid readers and writers. Reading expands your vocabulary and understanding of different communication styles, while writing sharpens your ability to express ideas clearly.

Conclusion: Communication is Your Superpower

In the UK, where effective communication often involves balancing directness with tact, mastering this skill can set you apart. Whether you're inspiring a team, persuading an audience, or resolving conflicts, your words have the power to drive change and create connections.

As you continue your journey to think, act, and win like a champion, remember this: the way you communicate can make the difference between a good result and a great one.

In the next chapter, we'll explore the critical role of time management in winning and how to maximise every moment without burning out. For now, ask yourself: What's one step you can take today to improve your communication?

Your words are your greatest tool—use them wisely

Chapter 5: Time Management – Winning the Race Against the Clock

Time is the great equaliser. No matter who you are or what you do, you have the same 24 hours in a day as everyone else. What separates winners from the rest is how they use those hours. In a fast-paced world like the UK, where balancing work, family, and personal goals is a constant juggling act, mastering time management is essential for success.

Winners understand that time is their most valuable resource. They don't waste it—they invest it wisely. This chapter will guide you through proven strategies to maximise your productivity, maintain focus, and achieve your goals without burning out.

The Value of Time

"Lost wealth can be regained, but lost time is gone forever."

The UK, with its bustling cities, competitive industries, and active social lives, often leaves people feeling like there's never enough time in the day. Yet, winners see time not as something to spend aimlessly but as an asset to be managed strategically.

Ask yourself: How do you currently spend your time? Do your daily actions align with your long-term goals, or are you stuck in the trap of busyness without progress?

Time management isn't about doing more—it's about doing what matters.

The Three Pillars of Time Management

1. **Prioritisation**
   Winners know how to separate what's urgent from what's important. In a world full of distractions, focusing on what truly matters is a superpower.
   - Use the **Eisenhower Matrix** to categorise tasks:
     - Urgent and important: Do these now.
     - Important but not urgent: Schedule time for these.
     - Urgent but not important: Delegate or minimise these.
     - Neither urgent nor important: Eliminate these.
   - Example: Instead of reacting to every email immediately, block out time to handle important messages in one focused session.

2. **Efficiency**
   Winners find ways to achieve more in less time. This doesn't mean cutting corners—it means working smarter, not harder.
   - **Batch similar tasks** to reduce context-switching. For example, reply to emails, make phone calls, or complete admin work in one dedicated block.
   - Adopt the **Pomodoro Technique**: Work for 25 minutes, then take a 5-minute break. This method improves focus and prevents burnout.
3. **Boundaries**
   Time is finite, and winners protect it fiercely. Setting boundaries means learning to say no to tasks, commitments, or distractions that don't align with your priorities.
   - In the UK workplace, where "busy culture" can sometimes dominate, winners know that overcommitting leads to diminishing returns. Politely decline tasks that don't contribute to your goals or delegate them when possible.

Case Study: Richard Branson's Time Management

Sir Richard Branson, one of the UK's most iconic entrepreneurs, manages a global empire of Virgin companies while still finding time for family, travel, and philanthropy. His secret? Ruthless prioritisation and delegation.

Branson focuses only on tasks where he can add the most value, delegating the rest to trusted team members. He also schedules time for exercise and relaxation, understanding that a clear mind is essential for productivity.

His approach shows that time management isn't just about work—it's about creating balance to achieve sustainable success.

Common Time Wasters and How to Avoid Them

1. **Procrastination**
   Putting off tasks often leads to stress and lower-quality work. Winners overcome procrastination by:
   - Breaking large tasks into smaller, manageable steps.
   - Setting deadlines, even for tasks without external time constraints.
   - Rewarding themselves for completing difficult tasks.

2. **Multitasking**
   Studies show that multitasking reduces efficiency and increases mistakes. Instead, focus on one task at a time to achieve better results.
3. **Distractions**
   In the digital age, distractions like social media, emails, and constant notifications are everywhere. Combat this by:
   - Turning off non-essential notifications.
   - Using tools like Focus Mode or apps like Freedom to block distracting sites during work.
   - Creating a dedicated workspace free from interruptions.
4. **Overcommitting**
   Saying yes to everything spreads your time and energy too thin. Winners are selective with their commitments, ensuring their focus remains on what truly matters.

Time Management for Work-Life Balance in the UK

In the UK, where long working hours and commutes are common, achieving work-life balance can feel like an uphill battle.

However, winners understand that balance is key to sustained success.

1. **Set Clear Work Hours**
   If you work remotely or have flexible hours, establish boundaries around your work time. Avoid letting work bleed into personal time.
2. **Schedule Personal Time**
   Just as you'd schedule a meeting, block out time for family, exercise, or hobbies. These activities recharge your energy and improve overall productivity.
3. **Take Advantage of Downtime**
   Use commuting time to listen to audiobooks, catch up on podcasts, or reflect on your goals. Make even your "idle" moments productive.
4. **Use Technology Wisely**
   Apps like Google Calendar, Todoist, or Notion can help you stay organised and on track. In the UK, where train delays and unexpected disruptions can affect schedules, having a digital plan makes it easier to adapt.

Practical Time Management Tools and Techniques

1. **The 80/20 Rule (Pareto Principle)**
   80% of your results come from 20% of your efforts. Identify the tasks that deliver the most value and focus your energy there.
   - Example: If networking generates most of your business leads, prioritise it over less impactful activities.
2. **Daily Planning**
   Start each day by listing your top three priorities. These are your "must-dos" for the day. Completing them gives you a sense of accomplishment and keeps you moving towards your goals.
3. **Time Blocking**
   Assign specific time slots to tasks or activities. This prevents over-scheduling and ensures you dedicate enough time to important projects.
   - Example: Block 9–11 am for deep work, 2–3 pm for meetings, and 4–5 pm for admin tasks.
4. **Reflection and Adjustment**
   At the end of each week, review how you spent your time. Identify areas where you can improve and adjust your strategy for the following week.

Action Steps: Take Control of Your Time

1. **Audit Your Time**
   For one week, track how you spend your time in 30-minute intervals. Identify patterns, time-wasters, and opportunities for improvement.
2. **Create a Weekly Plan**
   Every Sunday evening, plan your week ahead. Set priorities, schedule important tasks, and leave room for flexibility.
3. **Eliminate One Time-Waster**
   Identify one habit or activity that consumes time without adding value (e.g., excessive scrolling on social media). Replace it with a more productive or fulfilling activity.
4. **Focus on Quality Over Quantity**
   Remember, it's not about how many hours you work but how effectively you use them. Prioritise meaningful tasks over busywork.

Conclusion: Time is Your Greatest Asset

Time management is about more than squeezing as much as possible into your day—it's about aligning your time with your values and goals. Winners understand that how you spend your time defines your success, your relationships, and ultimately your life.

In the next chapter, we'll dive into the habits and routines of winners—daily practices that create consistency and drive long-term success. For now, reflect on this: What's one change you can make today to better manage your time?

The clock is ticking—use it wisely.

Chapter 6: The Power of Habits – Daily Routines That Drive Success

Success is not built in a day—it's the result of consistent actions over time. Habits are the foundation of this consistency. They shape our behaviour, influence our mindset, and determine how we spend our time. Winners understand the power of habits and use them to create a life that aligns with their goals.

In the UK, where the rhythm of daily life often revolves around balancing work, family, and personal pursuits, cultivating effective habits can be the difference between thriving and just getting by. This chapter explores how to build winning habits, break bad ones, and design daily routines that set you up for success.

Why Habits Matter

"Success is the sum of small efforts repeated day in and day out." – Robert Collier

Habits are the autopilot of your life. Research shows that nearly 40% of our daily actions are habitual. This means that much of what we do is driven by routines rather than conscious decisions.

The question is: Are your habits helping or hindering you? Winners take control of their habits to ensure they work in their favour. From early morning rituals to evening wind-downs, they structure their day with purposeful actions that compound into success over time.

The Science of Habit Formation

Habits follow a three-step loop, as explained by Charles Duhigg in *The Power of Habit*:

1. **Cue**: A trigger that initiates the habit. This could be a time of day, an emotion, or an external event (e.g., your alarm ringing in the morning).
2. **Routine**: The behaviour itself. This is the habit you want to form or change.
3. **Reward**: The benefit you receive from completing the habit, which reinforces the behaviour.

Understanding this loop is the key to building new habits or breaking old ones. For example:

- **Cue**: Seeing your running shoes by the door.
- **Routine**: Going for a jog.
- **Reward**: The feeling of accomplishment and increased energy afterward.

Building Winning Habits

1. **Start Small**
   In the UK, where life often feels busy and fast-paced, it's tempting to aim for big changes all at once. However, small, incremental changes are more sustainable.
   - Example: If you want to read more, start with just 10 minutes a day rather than trying to finish a book in a week.
2. **Stack Habits**
   Habit stacking involves attaching a new habit to an existing one. This makes it easier to incorporate the new behaviour into your routine.
   - Example: After brushing your teeth in the morning, spend two minutes journaling or planning your day.
3. **Make It Easy**
   Reduce friction for positive habits and increase friction for negative ones.
   - Example: If you want to eat healthier, prepare meals in advance so that nutritious options are readily available.

4. **Track Your Progress**
   Winners track their habits to stay accountable and measure improvement. Use a journal, app, or calendar to log your progress.
   - Example: Tick off each day you complete a habit like exercising or meditating. Over time, the visual record becomes a motivator to keep going.
5. **Celebrate Small Wins**
   Reinforce your habits by rewarding yourself for consistency. The reward doesn't need to be extravagant—it could be as simple as enjoying a cup of tea after completing a task.

Breaking Bad Habits

1. **Identify the Cue**
   The first step to breaking a bad habit is understanding what triggers it. Is it boredom, stress, or a specific time of day?
   - Example: If you tend to snack mindlessly in the evening, the cue might be sitting on the sofa watching TV.

2. **Replace the Routine**
   Habits can't simply be eliminated; they need to be replaced. Find a positive alternative that satisfies the same need.
   - Example: Instead of snacking, try drinking herbal tea or doing a quick stretching routine.
3. **Increase Friction**
   Make bad habits harder to engage in.
   - Example: If you want to spend less time on social media, delete the apps from your phone or set time limits using apps like Screen Time.
4. **Get Support**
   Share your goals with friends or family who can hold you accountable. The UK's community culture offers plenty of opportunities for group support, whether it's joining a fitness class or participating in local events.

Morning Routines of Winners

The morning sets the tone for the rest of the day. Many successful people in the UK and beyond swear by their morning routines as a cornerstone of their success. Here's a typical winning morning routine:

1. **Wake Up Early**
   Waking up early provides quiet, uninterrupted time to focus on yourself before the demands of the day take over.
2. **Hydrate**
   Start the day with a glass of water to rehydrate after sleep. This simple habit boosts energy and mental clarity.
3. **Exercise or Stretch**
   Physical activity in the morning improves mood and increases focus throughout the day. It doesn't have to be a full workout—10 minutes of yoga or a brisk walk suffices.
4. **Plan Your Day**
   Use a planner or journal to outline your top priorities for the day. This ensures you stay focused on what matters most.
5. **Practice Gratitude**
   Reflect on three things you're grateful for. This habit cultivates a positive mindset and helps you approach the day with optimism.

Evening Routines for Rest and Recovery

Just as mornings set the tone for the day, evenings are crucial for winding down and preparing for tomorrow. A good evening routine promotes restful sleep and mental clarity.

1. **Limit Screen Time**
   Reduce exposure to screens an hour before bed. The blue light emitted by devices disrupts melatonin production, affecting sleep quality.
2. **Reflect on Your Day**
   Spend a few minutes journaling or reviewing what went well and what could be improved. This habit encourages self-awareness and growth.
3. **Prepare for Tomorrow**
   Lay out clothes, pack your bag, or write your to-do list for the next day. This reduces morning stress and ensures you start the day with intention.
4. **Create a Relaxing Environment**
   In the UK, where the weather often encourages cosy evenings, create a calming atmosphere with soft lighting, a cup of tea, or a good book.

Case Study: James Dyson's Routine for Innovation

Sir James Dyson, the British inventor behind Dyson vacuum cleaners, credits his success to consistent habits of curiosity and problem-solving. Dyson spends time each day tinkering with ideas, testing prototypes, and reflecting on failures.

His habit of daily experimentation—combined with resilience and persistence—led to over 5,000 failed prototypes before creating his first successful vacuum cleaner. Dyson's story highlights the power of sticking to a routine, even when results aren't immediate.

Action Steps: Build Your Winning Routine

1. **Choose One Keystone Habit**
   Focus on developing one powerful habit that has a ripple effect on other areas of your life. For example, regular exercise often leads to better sleep, improved mood, and increased productivity.
2. **Track Your Progress**
   Use a habit tracker to log your consistency. In the UK, where many people love stationery, a physical tracker like a bullet journal can be both practical and enjoyable.

3. **Reflect Weekly**
   Take time each week to assess how your habits are serving you. Adjust your routines as needed to stay aligned with your goals.
4. **Be Patient**
   Habits take time to form. Studies suggest it takes an average of 66 days to establish a new habit, so don't give up if results aren't immediate.

Conclusion: Habits Shape Your Future

Your daily habits determine the trajectory of your life. Winners understand that small, consistent actions compound over time to create extraordinary results. By cultivating effective habits and eliminating those that hold you back, you can design a life that supports your ambitions.

In the next chapter, we'll explore the importance of resilience and how winners bounce back from setbacks stronger than ever. But for now, ask yourself: What's one habit you can start building today to move closer to your goals?

Your future self will thank you.

Chapter 7: Resilience – Bouncing Back Stronger Than Ever

Life is full of setbacks. From personal disappointments to professional failures, challenges are an inevitable part of the journey. What sets winners apart is not the absence of adversity but their ability to bounce back stronger. Resilience—the ability to recover and thrive in the face of difficulty—is a cornerstone of success.

In the UK, where the "Keep Calm and Carry On" mantra has become a symbol of enduring spirit, resilience is deeply ingrained in the culture. From overcoming historical challenges to navigating modern uncertainties, resilience is what helps individuals and communities rise above the odds. This chapter explores how to cultivate resilience and turn obstacles into stepping stones for growth.

The Importance of Resilience

"Success is not final; failure is not fatal: it is the courage to continue that counts." – Winston Churchill

Resilience isn't about avoiding challenges—it's about embracing them as opportunities for growth.

Winners see failures as feedback and setbacks as temporary. They understand that resilience isn't a trait you're born with; it's a skill you develop through experience, mindset, and practice.

Ask yourself: How do you respond to adversity? Do you retreat, or do you use it as a chance to adapt and improve?

The Mindset of Resilience

1. **Adopt a Growth Mindset**
   Winners believe that abilities can be developed through effort and learning. This mindset, popularised by psychologist Carol Dweck, helps people view challenges as opportunities to grow rather than as threats.
   - Example: Instead of saying, "I'm not good at this," say, "I'm not good at this *yet*."
2. **Focus on What You Can Control**
   Resilient individuals don't waste energy worrying about things they can't change. Instead, they focus on their actions, attitudes, and responses to challenges.
   - Example: If you lose a job, focus on updating your CV and networking rather than dwelling on the loss.

3. **Embrace Failure as Part of Success**
   Every failure carries a lesson. Winners see setbacks as part of the journey rather than the end of the road.
   - Example: James Dyson, a British inventor, faced over 5,000 failed prototypes before creating his revolutionary vacuum cleaner. His resilience turned failure into innovation.

Building Resilience

1. **Strengthen Your Support Network**
   Resilience isn't built alone. Surround yourself with supportive friends, family, or colleagues who can provide encouragement and perspective.
   - In the UK, community groups, sports clubs, or even a local pub can offer opportunities to connect with others and build relationships.
2. **Practice Self-Care**
   Taking care of your physical and mental health is essential for resilience. Exercise, a balanced diet, and adequate sleep improve your ability to cope with stress.

- Example: A brisk walk in one of the UK's many parks or countryside trails can do wonders for clearing your mind and boosting your mood.
3. **Reframe Adversity**
Resilient people reframe challenges as opportunities for growth.
    - Instead of thinking, "Why is this happening to me?" ask, "What can I learn from this?"
    - Example: If you miss out on a promotion, consider how you can improve your skills to succeed next time.
4. **Set Small, Achievable Goals**
Breaking big challenges into smaller, manageable steps helps you regain control and build momentum.
    - Example: If you're recovering from a personal loss, focus on simple daily goals, such as going for a walk or preparing a healthy meal.

Case Study: The UK Spirit of Resilience

One of the most iconic examples of resilience in the UK's history is the response to the Blitz during World War II. Despite nightly bombings, Londoners and other communities across the UK showed extraordinary courage and determination.

People adapted to the challenges by creating bomb shelters, volunteering for civil defence, and finding moments of joy amid the chaos, such as dancing or singing in underground stations. Their resilience not only helped them survive but also inspired future generations to face adversity with courage and unity.

Resilience in the Workplace

1. **Adapt to Change**
   The UK job market, like many others, is constantly evolving. Resilience in the workplace means being flexible and willing to learn new skills.
   - Example: If your industry is shifting toward digital technology, invest in online courses to stay competitive.
2. **Manage Stress Proactively**
   Workplace stress is a common challenge, but resilient employees know how to manage it effectively.

- Take short breaks during the day. Even stepping out for a cup of tea can help clear your mind.
- Use tools like time-blocking to manage your workload and prevent overwhelm.

3. **Seek Feedback and Grow**
   Resilient professionals view feedback as an opportunity to improve rather than as criticism.
   - Example: If a project doesn't go as planned, ask your manager for constructive feedback and use it to refine your approach.

Turning Setbacks into Comebacks

1. **Acknowledge Your Feelings**
   Resilience doesn't mean suppressing emotions. Allow yourself to feel disappointment, frustration, or sadness, but don't let those emotions define you.
2. **Take Action**
   Winners don't stay stuck in a problem—they take steps to solve it. Even small actions can help you regain a sense of control.

3. **Celebrate Progress**
   Resilience is built through incremental progress. Celebrate small wins along the way to keep your momentum going.
   - Example: If you're recovering from an injury, celebrate milestones like walking a certain distance or completing physiotherapy sessions.
4. **Visualise Your Comeback**
   Imagine yourself overcoming the challenge and succeeding. This mental rehearsal builds confidence and motivates you to keep going.

Practical Steps to Build Resilience

1. **Create a Gratitude Journal**
   Write down three things you're grateful for each day. This shifts your focus from what's going wrong to what's going right.
2. **Learn to Say No**
   Overcommitting can lead to burnout. Practice setting boundaries to protect your time and energy.
3. **Develop a Resilience Plan**
   Write down strategies for handling setbacks in key areas of your life, such as work, relationships, and health. Having a plan reduces stress when challenges arise.

4. **Seek Inspiration**
   Read books, watch documentaries, or listen to podcasts about individuals who've overcome adversity. Their stories can inspire and motivate you to keep going.

Conclusion: Resilience is a Skill, Not a Trait

Resilience is not about avoiding challenges—it's about facing them head-on and emerging stronger. Whether you're navigating personal difficulties, professional setbacks, or life's unpredictable twists, resilience gives you the strength to keep moving forward.

As you continue your journey to think and act like a winner, remember resilience isn't built in a day, but with practice, it becomes one of your greatest strengths.

In the next chapter, we'll explore the role of teamwork and collaboration in achieving success, and how winners build and lead exceptional teams. But for now, reflect on this: What's one challenge you've faced recently, and how can you use it to grow stronger?

The greatest comebacks begin with resilience.

Chapter 8: Teamwork – The Power of Collaboration

No winner succeeds alone. Behind every great achievement is a team—whether it's a group of colleagues, family members, or mentors—working together towards a shared goal. Teamwork amplifies individual strengths, creates a supportive environment, and drives collective success.

In the UK, where collaboration is often valued in workplaces, sports teams, and communities, understanding how to work effectively with others is a vital skill. From the camaraderie of football teams like Manchester City to the collective efforts of NHS workers, teamwork is a cornerstone of success in many fields. This chapter explores how winners build, lead, and thrive in exceptional teams.

Why Teamwork Matters

"Talent wins games, but teamwork and intelligence win championships." – Michael Jordan

Teamwork is about more than just dividing tasks—it's about synergy. When a team works together effectively, the combined result is greater than the sum of its parts.

In the UK, examples of successful teamwork are everywhere:

- The **British rowing team** winning Olympic gold by working in perfect harmony.
- The **emergency services** coordinating during crises.
- Local communities coming together to support charities or organise events.

Ask yourself: Are you contributing to your team's success, or are you holding back? Understanding your role in a team is the first step towards collaboration.

Key Traits of Winning Teams

1. **A Shared Vision**
   Successful teams align around a common goal. This clarity ensures everyone understands their purpose and how their contributions fit into the bigger picture.
   - Example: In the UK's education system, teachers, parents, and students work together to achieve academic success.

2. **Trust and Respect**
   Trust is the foundation of teamwork. Without it, communication breaks down, and collaboration suffers. Winners build trust by being reliable, transparent, and supportive.
   - Respect for diverse perspectives is also crucial. In the UK's multicultural society, successful teams embrace differences to foster creativity and innovation.
3. **Clear Roles and Responsibilities**
   Ambiguity leads to confusion. In winning teams, each member knows their role and takes ownership of their responsibilities.
   - Example: A football team functions effectively when each player knows their position, whether they're a striker, midfielder, or goalkeeper.
4. **Effective Communication**
   Open and honest communication ensures that ideas are shared, problems are addressed, and everyone feels heard.

> Example: British Airways' turnaround in the 1980s under Sir Colin Marshall highlighted the importance of communication. Marshall encouraged employees to share their ideas and concerns, leading to improved operations and morale.

5. **Adaptability**
   Winning teams are flexible and willing to adapt when circumstances change.
   - Example: During the COVID-19 pandemic, many UK businesses transitioned to remote working, demonstrating adaptability in challenging times.

How Winners Lead Teams

Leadership plays a critical role in teamwork. Great leaders inspire, guide, and support their teams, ensuring everyone works towards a shared goal.

1. **Lead by Example**
   Leaders set the tone for the team. If you want others to be hardworking, respectful, and committed, you must model those behaviours.

- Example: Gareth Southgate, England's football manager, leads with humility and composure, inspiring his players to follow suit.

2. **Empower Others**
Winners don't micromanage—they trust their team members to deliver. Empowering others builds confidence and encourages initiative.
    - In the UK, collaborative leadership styles are often preferred, where employees are given autonomy to make decisions.

3. **Provide Feedback and Recognition**
Constructive feedback helps individuals grow, while recognition boosts morale and motivation.
    - Example: A simple "thank you" or public acknowledgment of effort can make a significant difference in team dynamics.

4. **Resolve Conflicts Quickly**
Conflict is natural in any team, but winners address it promptly and constructively.
    - Example: In a professional setting, mediating disagreements with fairness and empathy helps maintain a positive environment.

Case Study: Team GB and the Power of Collaboration

Team GB's success at the London 2012 Olympics is a testament to the power of teamwork. The athletes weren't just supported by their coaches but also by nutritionists, physiotherapists, psychologists, and countless behind-the-scenes staff. Each team member played a crucial role in the collective success.

Their motto, "Better Together," highlighted the importance of collaboration and unity. This approach led to Team GB's most successful Olympic Games in over a century.

The Challenges of Teamwork and How to Overcome Them

1. **Miscommunication**
   Misunderstandings can lead to frustration and mistakes.
   - Solution: Encourage clear, concise communication. In the UK workplace, tools like Slack or Microsoft Teams can help streamline conversations.

2. **Lack of Accountability**
   When team members don't take responsibility, it affects the entire group.
   - Solution: Establish clear expectations and hold regular check-ins to ensure progress.
3. **Different Working Styles**
   People have unique ways of approaching tasks, which can cause friction.
   - Solution: Recognise and respect these differences. Encourage team members to play to their strengths while supporting others.
4. **Groupthink**
   Teams that avoid challenging ideas risk stagnation.
   - Solution: Create an environment where constructive criticism is welcomed. Encourage diverse perspectives to drive innovation.

Practical Steps to Improve Teamwork

1. **Foster Inclusivity**
   Make sure everyone feels valued and included, regardless of background or role. In the UK, where diversity is celebrated, inclusivity strengthens teams.

2. **Hold Regular Meetings**
   Regular team meetings ensure alignment and provide opportunities to address challenges. Keep meetings focused and action-oriented to respect everyone's time.
3. **Celebrate Team Achievements**
   Recognising collective wins boosts morale and reinforces a sense of unity.
   - Example: A team lunch or a simple shoutout during a meeting can go a long way.
4. **Invest in Team Building**
   Activities like retreats, workshops, or even pub quizzes can strengthen relationships and improve collaboration.

The Role of Individual Responsibility

While teamwork is about collective effort, individual responsibility is equally important. Each team member must:

- Deliver on their commitments.
- Communicate openly and honestly.
- Support their teammates, even when the going gets tough.

Ask yourself: Are you contributing your best to your team? If not, what can you improve?

Action Steps to Enhance Teamwork

1. **Identify Your Role**
   Reflect on your strengths and how they contribute to your team's goals. Discuss your role with your team leader to ensure clarity.
2. **Practice Active Listening**
   During team discussions, focus on truly understanding others' perspectives before responding.
3. **Show Appreciation**
   Thank your teammates for their efforts. Simple gestures of gratitude can strengthen relationships.
4. **Be a Problem Solver**
   Instead of pointing out problems, come to the table with solutions. This proactive mindset enhances team dynamics.

Conclusion: Together, We Achieve More

Teamwork is about leveraging the collective power of individuals to achieve something greater than anyone could alone. Whether you're working on a sports team, in a corporate office, or with a group of friends, collaboration is key to success.

As you continue your journey to think and act like a winner, remember that no one achieves greatness in isolation. Build strong, supportive teams, and you'll multiply your chances of success.

In the next chapter, we'll explore the importance of leadership and how winners inspire others to follow them. But for now, ask yourself: What's one step you can take to strengthen your team today?

Great things happen when we work together.

Chapter 9: Leadership – Inspiring Others to Follow

Leadership isn't about authority—it's about influence. Great leaders inspire, motivate, and guide others toward a shared vision. They earn respect not by demanding it, but by embodying the values and behaviours they expect from their team.

In the UK, leadership is woven into every aspect of society, from the corporate boardroom to grassroots community projects. Iconic figures like Sir Winston Churchill, Dame Anita Roddick, and Marcus Rashford have demonstrated that effective leadership is about more than personal success—it's about empowering others to achieve greatness. This chapter explores the principles of leadership and how winners inspire others to follow.

What Makes a Great Leader?

"Leadership is not about being in charge. It is about taking care of those in your charge." – Simon Sinek

Great leaders share common traits that enable them to inspire trust, foster collaboration, and drive success:

1. **Visionary Thinking**
   Leaders see the bigger picture and articulate a clear vision that inspires others.
   - Example: Sir Tim Berners-Lee, the British inventor of the World Wide Web, had a vision of a connected world.
   - His leadership in promoting open standards and collaboration changed the way we communicate and access information.
2. **Emotional Intelligence (EQ)**
   Understanding and managing emotions—both your own and others'—is key to effective leadership. Emotional intelligence fosters empathy, communication, and conflict resolution.
   - Example: In the UK, a culturally diverse workplace often benefits from leaders with high EQ, who can bridge gaps and create inclusive environments.
3. **Decisiveness**
   Leaders make tough decisions with confidence and clarity. While they seek input and consider options, they don't shy away from responsibility.

- Example: During the COVID-19 pandemic, many UK business leaders had to make rapid decisions to adapt to remote work and changing regulations.

4. **Integrity**
Trust is the foundation of leadership. Great leaders act with honesty, fairness, and consistency, earning the respect of those they lead.
    - Example: Marcus Rashford's campaign to provide free school meals for children during holidays showcased not just his leadership but also his moral integrity.

5. **Adaptability**
In a rapidly changing world, leaders must be flexible and open to new ideas.
    - Example: The shift to remote work across the UK highlighted the importance of leaders who could adapt quickly while supporting their teams.

Leadership Styles in the UK

Leadership isn't one-size-fits-all. Effective leaders adapt their style to suit the situation and the people they're leading.

1. **Transformational Leadership**
   Transformational leaders inspire and motivate others by creating a vision and encouraging innovation.
   - Example: Dame Anita Roddick, founder of The Body Shop, transformed the retail industry by championing ethical sourcing and environmental sustainability.
2. **Servant Leadership**
   Servant leaders prioritise the needs of their team, fostering collaboration and growth.
   - Example: NHS leaders often adopt a servant leadership approach, focusing on patient care and supporting frontline staff.
3. **Democratic Leadership**
   Democratic leaders involve their team in decision-making, fostering inclusivity and collective ownership of outcomes.
   - Example: In the UK workplace, team-based decision-making is common, especially in creative industries like advertising and media.
4. **Autocratic Leadership**
   Autocratic leaders make decisions independently, which can be effective in high-pressure or crisis situations.

- Example: In emergency services, such as the fire brigade, decisive, top-down leadership is essential for quick action.

5. **Laissez-Faire Leadership**
   Laissez-faire leaders provide guidance but give their team autonomy to make decisions and solve problems.
   - Example: Startups and tech firms in the UK often adopt this approach to foster innovation and independence.

How Winners Lead by Example

1. **Walk the Talk**
   Leaders set the standard for behaviour through their actions. If you expect hard work, honesty, and commitment from your team, you must embody those qualities yourself.
   - Example: Sir Alex Ferguson, one of the most successful football managers in UK history, was known for his discipline and dedication, which inspired his players to match his standards.

2. **Empower Others**
   Great leaders don't seek to control—they seek to empower. By trusting your team and giving them the tools they need to succeed, you create an environment where everyone thrives.
   - Example: Delegating tasks and encouraging professional development shows trust and builds confidence within your team.
3. **Provide Clear Direction**
   Leaders ensure their team understands the mission and their role in achieving it. Clear communication and consistent guidance prevent confusion and foster unity.
   - Example: During the London 2012 Olympics, Lord Sebastian Coe's leadership ensured that every volunteer, athlete, and organiser understood their contribution to the Games' success.
4. **Stay Calm Under Pressure**
   In challenging situations, leaders remain composed, offering reassurance and stability to their team.
   - Example: Winston Churchill's calm and inspiring speeches during World War II rallied the UK in its darkest hours.

Practical Leadership Skills

1. **Active Listening**
   Leaders who listen to their team members build trust and gain valuable insights.
   - Tip: During meetings, summarise what others say to ensure understanding and demonstrate engagement.
2. **Conflict Resolution**
   Addressing conflicts promptly and fairly ensures a positive team dynamic.
   - Tip: In disagreements, focus on the issue, not the person, and seek win-win solutions.
3. **Decision-Making**
   Weigh options carefully but don't over-analyse. Leaders must be decisive and confident in their choices.
   - Tip: Use the 80/20 rule: Gather enough information to make an informed decision without waiting for perfection.

4. **Motivating Others**
   Recognise and celebrate achievements to boost morale and motivation.
   - Tip: In the UK workplace, a simple thank-you email, or public acknowledgment of a team member's contributions can make a big impact.

Case Study: Jacinda Ardern's Leadership Style

Although not from the UK, Jacinda Ardern's leadership during her tenure as Prime Minister of New Zealand offers valuable lessons for leaders worldwide. Ardern's empathetic, inclusive, and decisive approach during crises—such as the Christchurch shootings and COVID-19 pandemic—earned her global respect.

Her ability to connect with people on a human level, combined with clear communication and decisive action, reflects the kind of leadership that resonates deeply in the UK's cultural and professional landscape.

Leadership Challenges and How to Overcome Them

1. **Resistance to Change**
   Teams often resist change, especially in traditional UK industries.
   - Solution: Communicate the benefits of change clearly and involve the team in the process.
2. **Maintaining Morale**
   Low morale can hinder productivity and collaboration.
   - Solution: Recognise achievements, address concerns openly, and provide support during tough times.
3. **Balancing Authority and Approachability**
   Leaders must maintain authority while staying approachable.
   - Solution: Set clear boundaries but encourage open dialogue and feedback.

Action Steps to Develop Your Leadership Skills

1. **Seek Feedback**
   Ask colleagues or team members for feedback on your leadership style. Use their insights to improve.

2. **Invest in Personal Development**
   Read books, attend workshops, or take courses on leadership. In the UK, organisations like the Chartered Management Institute (CMI) offer valuable resources.
3. **Mentor Others**
   Supporting someone else's growth helps you refine your own leadership skills.
4. **Reflect Regularly**
   Set aside time to evaluate your leadership decisions and identify areas for improvement.

Conclusion: Leadership is About People

At its core, leadership is about serving others and helping them achieve their potential. Whether you're leading a team of thousands or simply guiding a small group, your ability to inspire, connect, and empower others will determine your success.

As you continue your journey to think and act like a winner, remember great leaders don't just create followers—they create more leaders.

In the next chapter, we'll explore how winners cultivate confidence and maintain self-belief, even in the face of doubt. But for now, reflect on this: What's one way you can lead more effectively in your current role?

True leadership inspires action—start today.

Chapter 10: Confidence – The Key to Self-Belief and Success

Confidence isn't something you're born with—it's something you build. It's the quiet assurance that you can handle whatever comes your way, even when the outcome is uncertain. Confidence allows winners to take risks, push boundaries, and stay resilient in the face of setbacks.

In the UK, where a culture of modesty and understatement is often celebrated, confidence can sometimes be misunderstood as arrogance. However, true confidence is grounded in self-awareness and humility. It's about trusting your abilities without needing to boast. In this chapter, we'll explore how winners cultivate confidence and maintain self-belief, even in challenging situations.

Why Confidence Matters

"Whether you think you can, or you think you can't—you're right." — Henry Ford

Confidence is the foundation of success. It affects how you present yourself, how others perceive you, and how you respond to opportunities. Without confidence, even the most talented individuals can struggle to reach their full potential.

Ask yourself: How confident are you in your abilities? What holds you back from stepping into new opportunities or taking risks? Building confidence starts with recognising your strengths and taking consistent steps to reinforce them.

The Difference Between Confidence and Arrogance

True confidence is often quiet and unassuming. It's about believing in yourself without needing to prove anything to others. Arrogance, on the other hand, is a facade often used to mask insecurity.

In the UK, where humility is valued, it's important to strike the right balance. Confidence doesn't mean shouting about your achievements—it means owning them and using them to inspire others.

Building Confidence: The Winner's Approach

1. **Start with Self-Awareness**
   Confidence begins with knowing your strengths, weaknesses, and values. Self-awareness allows you to set realistic goals and build on what you're already good at.
   - Example: If you're skilled at public speaking but struggle with time management, focus on improving the latter without neglecting the former.
2. **Set Small Goals and Achieve Them**
   Confidence grows through success. Start with small, achievable goals that allow you to build momentum.
   - Example: If you're nervous about networking, set a goal to attend one event and speak to two new people. Each success reinforces your belief in your abilities.

3. **Learn from Failure**
   Failure isn't the opposite of success—it's part of the journey. Winners see setbacks as opportunities to learn and grow.
   - Example: J.K. Rowling faced multiple rejections before *Harry Potter* became a global phenomenon. Her confidence in her story kept her going.
4. **Practice Positive Self-Talk**
   Your internal dialogue shapes your confidence. Replace negative thoughts with empowering affirmations.
   - Instead of saying, "I'm not good enough," say, "I'm learning and improving every day."
5. **Celebrate Your Achievements**
   Recognise and reward yourself for your accomplishments, no matter how small. This reinforces your sense of competence and motivates you to aim higher.
   - Example: Keep a "win journal" where you record daily or weekly successes, such as completing a task or overcoming a fear.

Confidence in Action: Practical Tips

1. **Body Language Matters**
   How you carry yourself affects how confident you feel and how others perceive you.
   - Stand tall, maintain eye contact, and use open gestures.
   - A firm handshake or a warm smile can convey confidence in the UK's professional and social settings.
2. **Dress for Success**
   Your appearance can influence your confidence. Wearing clothes that make you feel comfortable and professional helps you approach situations with self-assurance.
   - Example: In the UK workplace, a well-fitted suit or smart casual attire is often seen as a sign of confidence and competence.
3. **Prepare and Practise**
   Confidence comes from preparation. Whether it's a presentation, an interview, or a performance, thorough preparation reduces anxiety and boosts self-belief.
   - Example: Practising a speech in front of friends or recording yourself can help you refine your delivery and feel more confident on the day.

4. **Step Out of Your Comfort Zone**
   Confidence grows when you push your boundaries. Taking small risks helps you realise you're capable of more than you thought.
   - Example: If you're afraid of public speaking, start by presenting in front of a small, supportive audience before tackling larger groups.

Confidence in the Workplace

1. **Speak Up in Meetings**
   Many people in the UK hesitate to share their ideas for fear of judgment. However, confident individuals contribute to discussions and offer solutions.
   - Tip: Start by preparing one key point to share in each meeting. Over time, it will feel more natural to speak up.
2. **Seek Feedback**
   Asking for feedback shows confidence in your ability to improve. It also demonstrates a willingness to grow, which is valued in UK workplaces.
   - Example: After a presentation, ask colleagues for constructive feedback and use it to refine your skills.

3. **Build Professional Relationships**
   Networking can feel intimidating, but confidence grows with practice.
   - Tip: Start with informal settings, such as networking events or casual office gatherings, and gradually expand your circle.

Case Study: Confidence in Sport – Andy Murray

Andy Murray, one of Britain's greatest tennis players, is a prime example of confidence in action. Despite facing setbacks early in his career, including criticism about his temperament and challenges with injuries, Murray persevered.

His victory at Wimbledon in 2013 ended a 77-year drought for British men in the tournament. This win wasn't just about physical skill—it was about mental strength and self-belief. Murray's confidence in his abilities, combined with relentless preparation, propelled him to the top of his game.

Overcoming Imposter Syndrome

Many high achievers struggle with imposter syndrome—the feeling that they don't deserve their success. In the UK, where modesty is often emphasised, this phenomenon can be especially prevalent.

1. **Recognise Your Achievements**
   Remind yourself of your qualifications, skills, and accomplishments.
2. **Focus on Facts, Not Feelings**
   Feelings of inadequacy aren't based on reality. List the objective evidence of your success to counter self-doubt.
3. **Share Your Experience**
   Talking to others about imposter syndrome often reveals that many people feel the same way.
4. **Seek Support**
   Mentors, coaches, or supportive colleagues can provide perspective and encouragement.

Action Steps to Boost Confidence

1. **Daily Affirmations**
   Start each day with a positive statement about yourself or your abilities.
   - Example: "I am capable of handling today's challenges."
2. **Practice Gratitude**
   Reflect on what you're grateful for to shift your focus from what's lacking to what's thriving.
3. **Learn a New Skill**
   Confidence grows when you challenge yourself to learn and master something new.
   - Example: Take a course or attend a workshop in an area you're curious about.
4. **Surround Yourself with Positivity**
   Spend time with people who uplift and encourage you.

Conclusion: Confidence is a Muscle

Confidence isn't a fixed trait—it's a skill you develop through consistent effort. Whether you're navigating personal challenges, pursuing professional goals, or stepping into the unknown, self-belief is your greatest ally.

As you continue your journey to think and act like a winner, remember confidence grows with every step forward. Trust yourself, embrace your strengths, and don't be afraid to shine.

In the next chapter, we'll explore how winners maintain focus and eliminate distractions to stay on track and achieve their goals. But for now, reflect on this: What's one step you can take today to boost your confidence?

Believe in yourself—the world will follow.

Chapter 11: Focus – The Power of Eliminating Distractions

In a world filled with constant notifications, endless to-do lists, and the fast pace of modern life, staying focused can feel like an impossible task. Yet, focus is what separates those who achieve their goals from those who merely dream about them. Winners understand that focus isn't about working harder—it's about working smarter by directing their energy toward what truly matters.

In the UK, where the balance of work, commuting, and family life often feels overwhelming, developing focus is especially important. This chapter explores how winners maintain their attention, block out distractions, and create the clarity needed to stay on track.

Why Focus Matters

"You will never reach your destination if you stop to throw stones at every dog that barks." – Winston Churchill

Focus is the ability to tune out distractions and zero in on your goals. It's the driving force behind productivity, creativity, and long-term success.

Without focus, even the most ambitious plans can fall apart.

Ask yourself: How often do you feel pulled in multiple directions, unable to make meaningful progress? Learning to focus is about reclaiming control over your time and energy.

The Science of Focus

Your brain is wired to focus on one task at a time. Multitasking, while often celebrated, is actually a myth—switching between tasks reduces productivity by up to 40%. Winners understand this and prioritise deep work, a concept popularised by author Cal Newport, which involves immersing yourself in a single, high-value task without distractions.

The Distraction Epidemic

1. **Technology Overload**
   In the UK, the average person checks their phone over 100 times a day. Notifications, emails, and social media are constant interruptions.
2. **Open-Plan Workspaces**
   Many UK workplaces use open-plan designs, which can lead to frequent interruptions and reduced concentration.

3. **Busy Culture**
   In a society that values productivity, being "busy" is often mistaken for being effective. However, busyness without focus leads to burnout, not success.

How Winners Cultivate Focus

1. **Clarify Your Priorities**
   Winners don't try to do everything—they focus on what matters most.
   - Example: Use the **Pareto Principle (80/20 Rule)** to identify the 20% of tasks that produce 80% of your results. Prioritise these tasks.
   - Tip: Start each day by identifying your top three priorities. These are your "must-dos."
2. **Eliminate Distractions**
   Create an environment that supports focus by removing common distractions.
   - Example: Turn off non-essential notifications on your phone. Use apps like Focus@Will or Freedom to block distracting websites during work hours.

- Tip: In the UK, where public transport is common, use commuting time for focused activities like reading or planning your day.

3. **Time Blocking**
Schedule specific blocks of time for focused work.
    - Example: Dedicate 9–11 am to deep work, 1–2 pm to emails, and 3–4 pm to meetings. Stick to these blocks as much as possible.
    - Tip: Use a planner or digital tools like Google Calendar to organise your time.

4. **Practice Mindfulness**
Mindfulness improves your ability to concentrate and reduces stress.
    - Example: Spend 5–10 minutes meditating each morning. Apps like Headspace and Calm, popular in the UK, can guide you.
    - Tip: When you feel distracted, take a moment to breathe deeply and refocus on the task at hand.

The Power of Saying No

One of the most effective ways to maintain focus is learning to say no. Winners don't agree to every request—they guard their time fiercely.

1. **Set Boundaries**
   Politely decline tasks or commitments that don't align with your goals.
   - Example: In the UK workplace, it's common to feel pressured to attend every meeting. If a meeting isn't essential, request a summary instead.
2. **Delegate**
   Focus on what you do best and delegate the rest.
   - Example: If you're a manager, delegate routine tasks to team members, freeing up time for strategic work.
3. **Be Honest**
   Saying no doesn't mean being rude—it means being clear about your priorities.
   - Example: "I'd love to help, but I'm currently focused on a project with a tight deadline."

Case Study: Focus in Sport – Jessica Ennis-Hill

Jessica Ennis-Hill, one of Britain's most celebrated athletes, is a shining example of focus. As a heptathlete, Ennis-Hill had to train across seven disciplines, each requiring precision and dedication. Her ability to focus on incremental improvements in every event led to her winning Olympic gold at London 2012.

Ennis-Hill's success wasn't just about physical talent—it was about mental discipline. She prioritised her training, eliminated distractions, and stayed committed to her long-term vision, even after setbacks like injuries.

Creating a Focus-Friendly Environment

1. **Designate a Dedicated Workspace**
   Whether you work from home or in an office, create a space free from distractions.
   - Example: In the UK, many people use spare rooms or garden offices as dedicated workspaces.
2. **Use Noise-Cancelling Tools**
   Block out distractions with noise-cancelling headphones or apps that play ambient sounds.

- Tip: Focus-friendly playlists are available on platforms like Spotify and Apple Music.
3. **Declutter Your Space**
   A tidy environment promotes a tidy mind.
   - Example: Keep only essential items on your desk to reduce visual distractions.

Maintaining Focus in the Long Term

1. **Take Regular Breaks**
   The brain can only maintain peak focus for 90–120 minutes.
   - Tip: Use the **Pomodoro Technique**: Work for 25 minutes, then take a 5-minute break. Every four cycles, take a longer 15–30-minute break.
2. **Reflect and Adjust**
   At the end of each day, review your progress. Identify what worked well and what didn't and adjust your approach accordingly.
   - Example: If you find afternoon energy dips, schedule lighter tasks during that time.

3. **Reward Yourself**
   Celebrate milestones to stay motivated.
   - Example: Treat yourself to a favourite meal or activity after completing a major project.

Action Steps to Improve Focus

1. **Audit Your Time**
   Track how you spend your time for a week. Identify distractions and time-wasters, then take steps to eliminate them.
2. **Start a Daily Focus Practice**
   Spend the first 10 minutes of your workday planning your priorities. This ensures you start with intention.
3. **Limit Multitasking**
   Commit to completing one task at a time. Use a timer if necessary to stay focused.
4. **Establish Tech-Free Zones**
   Create spaces where you disconnect from screens, such as the dining table or bedroom.

Conclusion: Focus is Your Superpower

In today's fast-paced world, the ability to focus is a rare and valuable skill. By eliminating distractions, prioritising effectively, and creating routines that support deep work, you can accomplish more in less time.

As you continue your journey to think and act like a winner, remember focus is about quality, not quantity. Stay present, stay committed, and the results will follow.

In the next chapter, we'll explore how winners balance ambition with well-being, ensuring long-term success without sacrificing health or happiness. But for now, ask yourself: What's one distraction you can eliminate today to improve your focus?

Success starts with attention—make yours count.

Chapter 12: Balance – The Key to Sustained Success and Well-Being

Ambition drives us to achieve great things, but without balance, even the most successful individuals risk burnout, dissatisfaction, or a loss of perspective. Balance isn't about dividing your time equally between work, family, and personal goals—it's about aligning your actions with your values and creating a life that feels fulfilling and sustainable.

In the UK, where work-life balance is often a hot topic, achieving harmony between ambition and well-being is more important than ever. Whether it's navigating long commutes, demanding jobs, or family responsibilities, finding balance requires intentional choices and a willingness to prioritise what truly matters. This chapter explores how winners maintain balance, ensuring they thrive in all areas of life.

Why Balance Matters

"Happiness is not a matter of intensity but of balance, order, rhythm, and harmony." – Thomas Merton

Without balance, success can come at a cost. Winners understand that true achievement isn't just about reaching professional goals—it's about creating a life that's rich in purpose, relationships, and well-being.

Ask yourself: Are you prioritising the things that matter most to you? Or are you stuck in a cycle of constant busyness, neglecting key aspects of your life?

Balance is about making space for all the things that bring you joy and fulfilment.

The Challenge of Balance in the UK

1. **Long Working Hours**
   Many professionals in the UK struggle with extended working hours, especially in competitive industries like finance and law.
   - Example: Studies show that employees in the UK often work unpaid overtime, sacrificing personal time for career advancement.
2. **The Commute**
   With an average daily commute of 59 minutes, UK workers often lose valuable time to travel, particularly in urban areas like London.

3. **Digital Overload**
   Remote working and constant connectivity make it harder to switch off, blurring the lines between work and personal life.

How Winners Find Balance

1. **Define Your Priorities**
   Winners are clear about what matters most to them, whether it's family, health, career, or personal growth.
   - Tip: Write down your top five priorities and evaluate how much time you're currently dedicating to each. Adjust accordingly to align your actions with your values.
2. **Set Boundaries**
   Maintaining balance requires boundaries around work, technology, and other demands on your time.
   - Example: In the UK, the "right to disconnect" is gaining traction, encouraging employees to set limits on after-hours work communication.

3. **Create Non-Negotiables**
   Identify activities that are essential for your well-being and make them non-negotiable.
   - Example: Commit to weekly family dinners, a daily walk in the park, or attending a fitness class.
4. **Practice Time Management**
   Effective time management helps you fit more into your day without feeling overwhelmed.
   - Tip: Use tools like Google Calendar or a planner to schedule time for work, relaxation, and personal goals.

Balancing Ambition with Self-Care

1. **Physical Health**
   Winners prioritise their health, understanding that a strong body supports a sharp mind.
   - Example: Incorporate regular exercise into your routine, whether it's a morning jog, yoga, or a local football match.
   - Tip: The NHS recommends at least 150 minutes of moderate activity per week—use this as a benchmark for your fitness goals.

2. **Mental Health**
   Mental well-being is just as important as physical health. Taking time to rest, reflect, and recharge helps you stay resilient.
   - Tip: Practice mindfulness or meditation daily. Apps like Calm and Headspace, popular in the UK, can help you get started.
   - Example: Spend time in nature—whether it's a walk in the countryside or a visit to a nearby green space—to boost your mood and reduce stress.
3. **Sleep**
   Sleep is often sacrificed in the name of productivity, but winners know that quality rest is essential for peak performance.
   - Tip: Establish a bedtime routine, avoid screens before bed, and aim for 7–9 hours of sleep each night.

Balancing Work and Family Life

1. **Be Present**
   When spending time with family, focus on being fully present.
   - Example: Put your phone away during meals and engage in meaningful conversations.

2. **Plan Family Activities**
   Schedule regular activities that everyone can enjoy, from weekend outings to simple movie nights at home.
   - Tip: In the UK, explore National Trust properties, local parks, or cultural events for affordable family outings.
3. **Involve Your Family in Your Goals**
   Share your ambitions with your family and involve them in your journey.
   - Example: If you're training for a marathon, encourage your family to join you for practice runs or attend the event to cheer you on.

Balance in the Workplace

1. **Use Your Annual Leave**
   Many UK employees don't take their full holiday entitlement, missing opportunities to rest and recharge.
   - Tip: Plan your holidays in advance to ensure you take regular breaks throughout the year.
2. **Flexible Working**
   Take advantage of flexible working options, such as remote work or adjusted hours, to create a schedule that suits your lifestyle.

3. **Delegate and Automate**
   Avoid overloading yourself by delegating tasks or using technology to streamline your workflow.
   - Example: Use apps like Trello or Asana to manage tasks efficiently.

Case Study: Balancing Ambition and Well-Being – Emma Raducanu

British tennis star Emma Raducanu rose to fame after winning the US Open in 2021. While her rapid success brought immense pressure, Raducanu has prioritised maintaining balance in her life. She emphasises the importance of mental health, takes breaks to recharge, and ensures that her career ambitions align with her personal well-being.

Her approach reminds us that even at the highest levels of success, balance is essential for sustainability.

Action Steps to Create Balance

1. **Conduct a Life Audit**
   Assess how much time you're spending on work, family, health, and personal goals. Identify areas where you need to make adjustments.

2. **Establish a Morning Routine**
   Start your day with activities that energise and centre you, such as exercise, journaling, or meditation.
3. **Schedule Downtime**
   Block out time in your calendar for relaxation and hobbies. Treat this time as sacred as a work meeting.
4. **Communicate Your Needs**
   Talk to your employer, family, or friends about your boundaries and priorities. Clear communication ensures they understand and support your efforts to maintain balance.

Conclusion: Balance is a Journey, Not a Destination

Achieving balance doesn't mean everything in your life will be perfectly aligned at all times. It's a dynamic process that requires regular reflection, adjustment, and self-awareness.

Winners understand that balance is key to long-term success and happiness—they know when to push forward and when to step back.

As you continue your journey to think and act like a winner, remember balance isn't a luxury—it's a necessity.

Prioritise your well-being, nurture your relationships, and align your actions with your values.

In the next chapter, we'll explore how winners stay motivated and sustain their drive over the long haul. But for now, reflect on this: What's one change you can make today to bring more balance into your life?

Success without balance isn't success—it's compromise. Choose wisely.

Chapter 13: Motivation – Staying Driven for the Long Haul

Motivation is the fuel that keeps you moving toward your goals. It's the spark that gets you started and the force that helps you push through challenges. However, motivation isn't always constant—it ebbs and flows. Winners understand this and develop strategies to sustain their drive over the long haul.

In the UK, where daily life often involves balancing work pressures, personal responsibilities, and the unpredictable British weather, staying motivated can be particularly challenging. This chapter explores how to cultivate and maintain motivation, even when external circumstances threaten to derail your progress.

Why Motivation Matters

"Success is the sum of small efforts repeated day in and day out." – Robert Collier

Motivation is the bridge between your dreams and your actions. Without it, even the most well-laid plans remain unfulfilled. Yet, motivation isn't something you simply *have*—it's something you create and nurture.

Ask yourself: What motivates you? Is it personal achievement, providing for your family, or making a difference in the world? Understanding your "why" is the first step to sustaining your drive.

The Two Types of Motivation

1. **Intrinsic Motivation**
   This comes from within—your personal values, passions, and sense of purpose.
   - Example: A teacher in the UK might feel intrinsically motivated by a desire to help students succeed and make a positive impact on their lives.
2. **Extrinsic Motivation**
   This comes from external rewards, such as money, recognition, or promotions.
   - Example: A salesperson might feel motivated by hitting targets and earning bonuses.

Winners often combine both types, using intrinsic motivation for long-term sustainability and extrinsic rewards for short-term boosts.

How Winners Stay Motivated

1. **Set Meaningful Goals**
   Goals that align with your values are more likely to keep you motivated. Break big goals into smaller, manageable milestones to maintain momentum.
   - Example: If your goal is to run the London Marathon, start with smaller targets like completing a 5K, then a 10K, and so on.
2. **Visualise Success**
   Winners use visualisation to keep their goals front and centre. Imagine how it will feel to achieve your goal and the impact it will have on your life.
   - Example: Create a vision board with images and quotes that represent your aspirations, such as owning a home, writing a book, or starting a business.
3. **Celebrate Progress**
   Recognising and celebrating small wins reinforces your motivation and builds confidence.
   - Example: Treat yourself to a dinner out or a day trip after reaching a milestone, such as completing a challenging work project.

4. **Stay Accountable**
   Share your goals with a trusted friend, mentor, or group. Accountability partners can encourage you when your motivation dips.
   - Example: Join a local running club or professional organisation in the UK to stay motivated and connected.

Overcoming Common Motivation Challenges

1. **Procrastination**
   Delaying tasks can drain your motivation.
   - Solution: Use the **two-minute rule**—start any task by committing just two minutes to it. Once you begin, you're more likely to continue.
2. **Burnout**
   Overworking can lead to exhaustion and loss of motivation.
   - Solution: Schedule regular breaks and prioritise self-care. For example, take a long weekend in the Lake District or a day off to unwind.

3. **Lack of Visible Progress**
   Slow progress can feel discouraging.
   - Solution: Track your achievements to remind yourself how far you've come. Use apps like Strava for fitness goals or project management tools like Trello for work.
4. **Negative Self-Talk**
   Doubts and fears can sabotage motivation.
   - Solution: Replace negative thoughts with positive affirmations. Instead of saying, "I can't do this," tell yourself, "I'm capable of figuring this out."

Case Study: Sir Mo Farah and Sustained Motivation

Sir Mo Farah, one of the UK's greatest athletes, is a prime example of sustained motivation. From winning gold medals at the Olympics to setting records in long-distance running, Farah's success is built on a relentless work ethic and an unshakable belief in his abilities. Farah credits his motivation to a combination of intrinsic and extrinsic factors: his love for running, his desire to make his family proud, and the external recognition of his achievements. Even in the face of setbacks and injuries, Farah stays motivated by focusing on his goals and the joy of competing.

Practical Tips to Boost Motivation

1. **Create a Daily Routine**
   Structure your day to include time for your goals. A consistent routine reduces decision fatigue and keeps you on track.
   - Example: Dedicate 30 minutes each morning to a specific task, such as writing, exercising, or learning a new skill.
2. **Surround Yourself with Positive Influences**
   The people you spend time with can either inspire or drain you. Choose friends, colleagues, and mentors who uplift and encourage you.
   - Tip: Attend events or join groups in the UK that align with your interests, such as creative workshops or business networking events.
3. **Find Your Motivation Triggers**
   Identify what inspires you and use it to reignite your drive.
   - Example: Listen to a motivational podcast, watch a TED Talk, or read about successful individuals who started where you are.
4. **Reward Yourself**
   Incentives can provide short-term motivation to complete tasks.

- Example: Treat yourself to a West End show or a weekend getaway after achieving a significant milestone.

The Role of Resilience in Motivation

Resilience and motivation go hand in hand. When setbacks occur, resilient individuals find ways to adapt and maintain their drive.

1. **Reframe Challenges**
   Instead of viewing obstacles as failures, see them as opportunities to learn and grow.
2. **Stay Flexible**
   Adjust your goals and strategies as needed. Flexibility ensures you stay motivated even when circumstances change.
3. **Keep Your "Why" in Mind**
   Remind yourself of your purpose when motivation wanes. Write it down and place it somewhere visible, such as your desk or fridge.

Action Steps to Sustain Motivation

1. **Define Your Why**
   Reflect on the deeper reasons behind your goals. Write them down and revisit them regularly.

2. **Set SMART Goals**
   Make your goals Specific, Measurable, Achievable, Relevant, and Time-bound.
3. **Track Your Progress**
   Use journals, apps, or charts to monitor your achievements. Seeing tangible results keeps you motivated.
4. **Reconnect with Nature**
   Spending time outdoors can boost your mood and motivation. Take a walk in a local park, hike in the Peak District, or visit the coast for a dose of inspiration.

Conclusion: Motivation is a Muscle

Motivation isn't something you find—it's something you build. By understanding your "why," setting meaningful goals, and taking consistent action, you can sustain your drive over the long haul. Winners don't rely on fleeting bursts of enthusiasm; they cultivate habits and mindsets that keep them motivated every day.

As you continue your journey to think and act like a winner, remember motivation is a choice. Stay focused, stay resilient, and keep moving forward.

In the next chapter, we'll explore the importance of gratitude and how cultivating it can transform your perspective and fuel your success.

But for now, ask yourself: What's one small action you can take today to reignite your motivation?

Success begins with a single step—take yours now.

Chapter 14: Gratitude – The Transformative Power of Appreciation

Gratitude is more than saying "thank you"—it's a way of seeing the world. It shifts your focus from what you lack to what you have, helping you appreciate the blessings in your life, no matter how small. For winners, gratitude isn't just an emotion—it's a practice that fuels positivity, strengthens relationships, and fosters resilience.

In the UK, where a cup of tea is often seen as the antidote to life's stresses, gratitude offers a similarly comforting and grounding effect. From the charm of British countryside walks to shared moments with loved ones, cultivating gratitude can help you find joy in the everyday. This chapter explores how embracing gratitude can transform your perspective and supercharge your success.

Why Gratitude Matters

"It is not happiness that makes us grateful, but gratefulness that makes us happy." – David Steindl-Rast

Gratitude rewires your brain to focus on the positive. Studies show that practising gratitude improves mental health, boosts happiness, and strengthens relationships.

It's the secret weapon of many winners, helping them stay grounded and motivated through life's ups and downs.

Ask yourself: How often do you stop to appreciate what you have? Gratitude isn't about ignoring challenges—it's about recognising the good that exists alongside them.

The Science of Gratitude

Practising gratitude activates the brain's reward system, releasing dopamine and serotonin—the chemicals responsible for happiness. Over time, this rewiring creates a more positive mindset, enhancing your ability to cope with stress and setbacks.

Gratitude in the UK: Finding Joy in Everyday Moments

1. **Appreciating Simple Pleasures**
   The UK's cultural traditions often celebrate small, meaningful moments—a cosy afternoon tea, a stroll through a local market, or a good conversation in the pub. Gratitude can start with recognising these simple joys.

2. **Seasonal Gratitude**
   From the beauty of bluebell woods in spring to the festive charm of Christmas markets, each season in the UK offers unique opportunities for gratitude.
   - Tip: Take a moment during your daily routine to notice the natural beauty around you, whether it's autumn leaves or the first daffodils of spring.

How Winners Cultivate Gratitude

1. **Keep a Gratitude Journal**
   Write down three things you're grateful for each day. They can be as big as a promotion or as small as enjoying a warm cup of tea.
   - Example: "I'm grateful for the sunny weather, a kind colleague, and the delicious homemade scones I had today."
2. **Express Gratitude to Others**
   Gratitude strengthens relationships. Make a habit of expressing appreciation to friends, family, and colleagues.
   - Example: In the workplace, a simple "Thank you for your support on this project" can build goodwill and morale.

3. **Reframe Challenges**
   Winners find gratitude even in difficult situations by focusing on what they've learned or how they've grown.
   - Example: If you missed out on a job opportunity, you might feel grateful for the chance to practice your interview skills or the feedback you received.
4. **Practice Mindfulness**
   Mindfulness enhances gratitude by helping you stay present and aware of your surroundings.
   - Tip: Spend a few minutes each day in quiet reflection, focusing on the things you're thankful for in that moment.

The Ripple Effect of Gratitude

1. **Improved Relationships**
   Gratitude fosters stronger connections by showing others they are valued.
   - Example: Writing a heartfelt thank-you note to a mentor or friend can deepen your bond.

2. **Enhanced Resilience**
   Gratitude helps you bounce back from adversity by reminding you of your strengths and support system.
   - Example: During challenging times, focusing on what's going well—such as supportive colleagues or good health—can provide a sense of stability.
3. **Greater Career Satisfaction**
   A grateful mindset can improve your attitude toward work, helping you see challenges as opportunities rather than obstacles.
   - Example: Be thankful for the chance to develop new skills, even if the task feels difficult in the moment.

Case Study: Captain Sir Tom Moore – A Life of Gratitude

Captain Sir Tom Moore became a national hero in the UK during the COVID-19 pandemic by raising over £32 million for NHS charities. Despite his advanced age and the challenges of lockdown, Captain Tom focused on gratitude, saying, "Tomorrow will be a good day."

His inspiring example shows that gratitude can be a powerful motivator, turning small actions into meaningful contributions. By appreciating life's blessings and giving back, he demonstrated how gratitude can create a positive ripple effect in the world.

Gratitude Practices to Try in the UK

1. **Morning Gratitude Ritual**
   Start your day by reflecting on one thing you're grateful for. This sets a positive tone for the rest of the day.
   - Tip: Pair this practice with your morning tea or coffee for a calming start.
2. **Nature Walks**
   The UK is full of stunning landscapes, from the Lake District to the Cotswolds. Spending time in nature can enhance your sense of gratitude.
   - Tip: During your walk, notice the details around you—the sound of birds, the scent of flowers, or the feel of the breeze.

3. **Family Gratitude Jar**
   Create a jar where family members can write down things they're grateful for. Read them together at the end of the week or month.
   - Example: "Grateful for a fun game night" or "Thankful for Mum's Sunday roast."
4. **Volunteer in Your Community**
   Giving back helps you appreciate your own blessings while making a positive impact.
   - Example: Volunteer at a local food bank, animal shelter, or charity shop.

Action Steps to Cultivate Gratitude

1. **Create a Gratitude List**
   Write down everything you're grateful for—big and small. Keep adding to the list over time.
2. **Share Your Gratitude**
   Each week, tell at least one person why you appreciate them.
3. **Reflect on the Positives**
   At the end of each day, reflect on three good things that happened, no matter how small.

4. **Practice Gratitude During Challenges**
   The next time you face a setback, ask yourself: What can I learn from this? What do I still have to be grateful for?

Conclusion: Gratitude is the Key to Abundance

Gratitude isn't just a feel-good practice—it's a powerful tool for transforming your mindset, relationships, and life. By focusing on what you have rather than what you lack, you create a sense of abundance that fuels success and happiness.

As you continue your journey to think and act like a winner, remember gratitude is a choice you make every day. Embrace it, and you'll find joy, resilience, and motivation in even the smallest moments.

In the next chapter, we'll explore how winners leave a legacy, using their success to inspire and uplift others. But for now, reflect on this: What's one thing you're grateful for today?

The more you practice gratitude, the more you'll find to be thankful for.

Chapter 15: Legacy – Creating a Lasting Impact

Success is not just about what you achieve in your lifetime—it's about the impact you leave behind. Your legacy is the story others tell about you when you're gone, shaped by the actions you take, the values you uphold, and the lives you touch. Winners don't just think about the present; they think about how their choices will resonate in the future.

In the UK, where history and tradition play a prominent role, the concept of legacy is deeply ingrained. From the contributions of innovators like Isambard Kingdom Brunel to the charitable efforts of Sir David Attenborough, leaving a legacy is about making a meaningful difference that extends beyond yourself. This chapter explores how winners build legacies that inspire, uplift, and endure.

Why Legacy Matters

"Plant trees under whose shade you do not plan to sit." – Nelson Henderson

A legacy isn't just about wealth or fame—it's about how you've shaped the world around you. Whether it's raising a family, mentoring others, or creating something of lasting value, your legacy reflects the ripple effect of your life's work.

Ask yourself: What do you want to be remembered for? What actions can you take today to create a positive impact tomorrow?

Types of Legacy

1. **Personal Legacy**
   This is the impact you leave on your family and close relationships. It includes the values you instil, the memories you create, and the love you share.
   - Example: Teaching your children kindness, resilience, and the importance of giving back.
2. **Professional Legacy**
   Your contributions to your career or industry—innovations, mentorship, or inspiring others through your work.
   - Example: Sir Tim Berners-Lee's invention of the World Wide Web has left an enduring legacy in technology.

3. **Social Legacy**
   The impact you make on your community or society as a whole, whether through activism, philanthropy, or volunteer work.
   - Example: Captain Sir Tom Moore's fundraising efforts for the NHS demonstrated how one person can inspire a nation.

How Winners Build a Legacy

1. **Live Your Values**
   A strong legacy starts with living authentically and consistently with your values.
   - Example: If you value environmental sustainability, take action by reducing waste, supporting green initiatives, or educating others about eco-friendly practices.
2. **Give Back to Your Community**
   Contributing to your community creates a lasting impact and strengthens social bonds.
   - Example: Volunteer at a local charity, mentor young professionals, or participate in initiatives like litter-picking in your neighbourhood.

3. **Create Something That Lasts**
   Whether it's a book, a business, or a charitable foundation, creating something tangible can ensure your legacy endures.
   - Example: Sir Richard Branson's Virgin Group embodies his legacy of innovation and adventure.
4. **Inspire and Mentor Others**
   Sharing your knowledge and experience helps others achieve their potential, extending your impact far beyond yourself.
   - Example: Offer guidance to colleagues, host workshops, or volunteer to speak at schools or community events.
5. **Focus on Relationships**
   A legacy isn't just about achievements—it's about the connections you build and the lives you touch.
   - Example: Spend quality time with loved ones, offer support during difficult times, and celebrate their successes.

Case Study: Dame Anita Roddick – A Legacy of Ethical Business

Dame Anita Roddick, founder of The Body Shop, left a profound legacy in the business world. She pioneered ethical and sustainable practices long before they became mainstream, proving that businesses could be a force for good.

Her commitment to fair trade, cruelty-free products, and environmental activism inspired a global movement and continues to influence the beauty industry today. Roddick's legacy demonstrates that success and social responsibility can go hand in hand.

Challenges of Building a Legacy and How to Overcome Them

1. **Fear of Starting Small**
   Many people believe they need to make grand gestures to leave a legacy.
   - Solution: Start with small, meaningful actions. Even simple acts of kindness or mentoring one person can create a ripple effect.

2. **Balancing Present and Future Goals**
   Focusing too much on legacy can lead to neglecting current responsibilities.
   - Solution: Integrate legacy-building into your daily life by aligning your actions with your values.
3. **Overcoming Self-Doubt**
   You might question whether your efforts will make a difference.
   - Solution: Remember that every positive action counts. You don't need to change the world—just impact one person at a time.

Practical Steps to Build Your Legacy in the UK

1. **Document Your Story**
   Write a journal, memoir, or blog to share your experiences, lessons, and insights.
   - Example: A grandparent documenting family recipes and traditions creates a legacy for future generations.
2. **Support Local Causes**
   Contribute to charities or organisations that align with your values.
   - Example: Support the Royal National Lifeboat Institution (RNLI) or the Woodland Trust to help preserve British heritage and nature.

3. **Educate and Advocate**
   Use your voice to raise awareness about issues you care about.
   - Example: Advocate for mental health awareness by participating in campaigns like Time to Change.
4. **Plant Seeds for the Future**
   Mentor, coach, or inspire others to achieve their potential.
   - Example: Offer career advice to students through schemes like the Prince's Trust.
5. **Create a Legacy Fund**
   Set aside resources to support a cause or initiative that's important to you.
   - Example: Establish a scholarship for underprivileged students in your local area.

Legacy in Everyday Life

1. **Be Kind**
   Acts of kindness leave a lasting impression on others.
   - Example: Helping a neighbour with their shopping or offering a compliment can brighten someone's day and contribute to your legacy.

2. **Teach What You Know**
   Sharing your knowledge ensures your skills and insights live on.
   - Example: Teach someone how to garden, cook, or fix a car—practical skills that can benefit them for life.
3. **Live with Purpose**
   Align your daily actions with your values to create a life that feels meaningful and fulfilling.
   - Example: If family is important to you, make time for regular gatherings and shared traditions.

Action Steps to Start Building Your Legacy Today

1. **Identify Your Values**
   Reflect on what matters most to you and how you want to be remembered.
2. **Set Legacy Goals**
   Decide what impact you want to make and outline steps to achieve it.
3. **Take Small Actions**
   Start with one small step toward building your legacy, such as mentoring someone, volunteering, or sharing your story.

4. **Reflect and Adjust**
   Periodically review your actions to ensure they align with the legacy you want to create.

Conclusion: Your Legacy Begins Now

Your legacy isn't something you leave behind—it's something you build every day. By living authentically, giving back, and inspiring others, you create a ripple effect that extends far beyond your lifetime.

As you continue your journey to think and act like a winner, remember: the choices you make today shape the impact you'll have tomorrow.

In the next chapter, we'll explore how winners embrace lifelong learning and growth to continually evolve and achieve greater heights. But for now, reflect on this: What's one action you can take today to start building your legacy?

Your legacy is your gift to the future—make it meaningful.

Chapter 16: Lifelong Learning – The Journey of Continuous Growth

Learning doesn't stop when formal education ends. Winners understand that growth is a lifelong journey, and the pursuit of knowledge is key to staying relevant, adaptable, and inspired. In a world that's constantly evolving, especially in the UK where industries and technology are advancing rapidly, the ability to learn, unlearn, and relearn is more valuable than ever.

From enrolling in courses at prestigious institutions like Oxford and Cambridge to exploring new hobbies or skills, lifelong learning empowers you to stay curious, challenge yourself, and achieve your fullest potential. This chapter explores how winners embrace continuous learning to fuel their success.

Why Lifelong Learning Matters

"Live as if you were to die tomorrow. Learn as if you were to live forever." – Mahatma Gandhi

In today's fast-paced world, staying stagnant is not an option. Lifelong learning keeps your mind sharp, opens new opportunities, and enhances personal and professional development.

Ask yourself: When was the last time you learned something new? Are you actively seeking knowledge, or are you relying on what you already know? Winners understand that growth requires stepping out of their comfort zone and embracing the unfamiliar.

The Benefits of Lifelong Learning

1. **Professional Growth**
   The UK job market is competitive, and upskilling is essential for career advancement. Lifelong learning helps you stay ahead of industry trends and stand out in your field.
   - Example: A teacher pursuing a new certification in digital learning can enhance their teaching methods and career prospects.
2. **Personal Fulfilment**
   Learning a new skill or exploring a passion enriches your life and boosts your confidence.
   - Example: Taking up photography, gardening, or learning a new language can bring joy and satisfaction.

3. **Adaptability**
   In a rapidly changing world, the ability to learn ensures you can adapt to new challenges and environments.
   - Example: During the COVID-19 pandemic, many UK professionals learned remote working tools like Zoom and Microsoft Teams to stay connected.
4. **Mental Agility**
   Lifelong learning keeps your brain active, improving memory and cognitive function as you age.
   - Tip: Engage in activities like puzzles, coding, or learning to play a musical instrument to challenge your mind.

How Winners Embrace Lifelong Learning

1. **Stay Curious**
   Winners cultivate a mindset of curiosity, always asking questions and seeking answers.
   - Example: Follow the latest developments in your industry by subscribing to relevant journals, blogs, or podcasts.

2. **Set Learning Goals**
   Approach learning with intention by setting clear goals.
   - Example: If you want to learn a new language, set a goal to complete a basic conversation course within six months.
3. **Leverage Technology**
   Online learning platforms like FutureLearn, Udemy, and Coursera make education accessible from anywhere in the UK.
   - Tip: Dedicate 20 minutes a day to an online course on a topic that interests you.
4. **Learn from Others**
   Mentorship, networking, and collaboration are powerful ways to gain new perspectives and skills.
   - Example: Join a professional group like the Chartered Institute of Personnel and Development (CIPD) to connect with peers and industry experts.

Case Study: David Attenborough – A Lifetime of Learning

Sir David Attenborough is a quintessential example of lifelong learning. Over decades, he has expanded his knowledge of the natural world and used it to educate and inspire millions. Even in his 90s, Attenborough continues to learn about new topics, such as climate change and renewable energy, ensuring his work remains relevant and impactful.

His legacy shows that curiosity and the pursuit of knowledge can enrich not only your life but also the lives of others.

Practical Ways to Start Lifelong Learning in the UK

1. **Take Evening or Weekend Classes**
   Many UK colleges and universities offer part-time courses for adults in areas like cooking, art, coding, or business skills.
   - Example: Check out courses offered by City Lit in London or the Open University for flexible learning options.

2. **Explore Local Resources**
   Libraries, museums, and community centres often host free or low-cost workshops and events.
   - Example: Attend a lecture at the British Library or a history talk at a local museum.
3. **Join Clubs or Societies**
   Social learning can be fun and rewarding.
   - Example: Join a book club, hiking group, or photography society to meet like-minded people while learning something new.
4. **Use Apps and Audiobooks**
   Technology makes it easy to learn on the go.
   - Example: Use apps like Duolingo to learn a new language or Audible to explore non-fiction books during your commute.

Lifelong Learning for Professional Growth

1. **Pursue Professional Qualifications**
   Many UK industries value certifications and continuous professional development (CPD).

- Example: Accountants can earn ACCA or CIMA qualifications to advance their careers.
2. **Attend Conferences and Workshops**
Networking events and industry seminars are great ways to stay updated and connect with experts.
    - Example: Attend events like the UK Business Show or Tech Week to learn from industry leaders.
3. **Read Widely**
Expand your knowledge by reading books, articles, and reports in your field.
    - Tip: Set a goal to read one industry-related book each month.

How to Overcome Barriers to Lifelong Learning

1. **Time Constraints**
Many people feel too busy to learn.
    - Solution: Break learning into small, manageable chunks, such as listening to a podcast during your commute or dedicating 15 minutes a day to an online course.

2. **Financial Limitations**
   Education can be expensive, but many free or low-cost options are available.
      - Solution: Explore free online courses, library resources, or community workshops.
3. **Fear of Failure**
   Trying something new can be intimidating.
      - Solution: Embrace a growth mindset and remind yourself that every expert was once a beginner.

Action Steps to Embrace Lifelong Learning

1. **Create a Learning Plan**
   Identify one skill or topic you want to focus on and outline how you'll approach it.
2. **Commit to Daily Learning**
   Dedicate at least 10 minutes a day to reading, practising, or exploring a new topic.
3. **Join a Community**
   Find a local group, online forum, or professional organisation to support your learning journey.
4. **Reflect on Your Progress**
   At the end of each week or month, review what you've learned and how it's benefiting your personal or professional life.

Conclusion: Learning is the Key to Unlimited Growth

Lifelong learning isn't just about acquiring knowledge—it's about staying curious, adaptable, and open to new experiences. In the UK, where opportunities for education and exploration abound, there's no better time to invest in your growth.

As you continue your journey to think and act like a winner, remember: the most successful people never stop learning. Whether it's mastering a new skill, gaining insights from others, or embracing new challenges, every step you take enriches your life and prepares you for the future.

In the next chapter, we'll explore how winners harness the power of mindfulness to stay grounded and focused in a busy world. But for now, reflect on this: What's one skill or topic you've always wanted to learn, and how can you start today?

Knowledge is power—keep growing.

Chapter 17: Mindfulness – Staying Grounded in a Busy World

In an age of constant notifications, fast-paced living, and endless demands, mindfulness has become more important than ever. Winners understand that success isn't just about pushing forward—it's also about being present, staying grounded, and finding clarity amidst the chaos. Mindfulness helps you focus, reduce stress, and approach challenges with a calm, clear mind.

In the UK, where long commutes, busy schedules, and unpredictable weather often add to life's pressures, mindfulness offers a way to reconnect with the moment and recharge. From practising meditation to simply enjoying a quiet moment with a cup of tea, mindfulness is about creating space for reflection and balance. This chapter explores how mindfulness can transform your life and help you thrive.

Why Mindfulness Matters

"You should sit in meditation for 20 minutes a day, unless you're too busy—then you should sit for an hour." – Zen Proverb

Mindfulness is the practice of paying attention to the present moment without judgment. It helps you focus on what truly matters, rather than getting lost in worries about the past or future. Research shows that mindfulness improves mental health, boosts productivity, and enhances overall well-being.

Ask yourself: How often do you feel fully present in your day-to-day life? Are you rushing through tasks, or are you taking time to savour the moment? Mindfulness is about slowing down and finding peace in the present.

The Benefits of Mindfulness

1. **Reduced Stress**
   Mindfulness lowers cortisol levels, helping you stay calm and composed during challenging times.
   - Example: Practising mindfulness during a stressful workday can help you handle meetings or deadlines with greater ease.
2. **Improved Focus**
   Being present enhances your ability to concentrate on tasks, leading to better results.

- Tip: Use mindfulness techniques to stay focused during long meetings or projects.
3. **Better Relationships**
Mindfulness fosters empathy and active listening, strengthening your connections with others.
    - Example: During a conversation, focus entirely on what the other person is saying instead of thinking about your response.
4. **Enhanced Resilience**
By accepting challenges without judgment, mindfulness helps you bounce back from setbacks more effectively.
    - Tip: When faced with failure, practise mindfulness to reflect on what you can learn rather than dwelling on the negative.

Mindfulness in the UK: Everyday Opportunities

1. **Tea Time as a Mindful Moment**
Tea is a quintessential part of British culture, and it offers a perfect opportunity to practise mindfulness.

- Tip: During your next tea break, focus on the warmth of the cup, the aroma of the tea, and the taste with each sip.

2. **Commutes as Mindful Journeys**

   Long commutes are a common part of UK life. Turn this time into a mindful experience by observing your surroundings or listening to calming music or a podcast.
   - Example: On a train journey, pay attention to the scenery outside the window or focus on your breathing.

3. **Mindful Walks**

   The UK's parks, countryside, and coastline provide ideal settings for mindfulness.
   - Tip: Take a slow, deliberate walk in a nearby green space, noticing the sounds, sights, and smells around you.

How Winners Practise Mindfulness

1. **Meditation**

   Meditation is a powerful tool for cultivating mindfulness. Even a few minutes a day can make a difference.

- Tip: Use apps like Calm or Headspace to guide your meditation practice. Start with 5–10 minutes and gradually increase.
2. **Breath Awareness**
Focusing on your breath anchors you to the present moment.
    - Tip: When you feel stressed, take a deep breath in for four counts, hold for four counts, and exhale for six counts. Repeat this cycle a few times.
3. **Mindful Eating**
Instead of rushing through meals, savour each bite and pay attention to the flavours and textures.
    - Example: During your next meal, put your fork down between bites and focus on the experience of eating.
4. **Gratitude Practice**
Combining mindfulness with gratitude helps you focus on the positive aspects of your life.
    - Tip: Spend a few minutes each evening reflecting on three things you're grateful for.

Case Study: Mindfulness in UK Healthcare

The NHS has embraced mindfulness as a tool to support mental health and well-being. Mindfulness-Based Cognitive Therapy (MBCT), developed in the UK, is used to help individuals manage depression, anxiety, and stress.

The success of MBCT highlights the transformative power of mindfulness in improving mental health, not only in clinical settings but also in everyday life.

Overcoming Common Challenges with Mindfulness

1. **I Don't Have Time**
   Many people feel too busy to practise mindfulness.
   - Solution: Start small. Even one minute of focused breathing or mindful observation can make a difference.
2. **I Can't Clear My Mind**
   Mindfulness isn't about stopping your thoughts—it's about observing them without judgment.
   - Solution: When your mind wanders, gently bring your focus back to your breath or the present moment.

3. **It Feels Unproductive**
   In a results-driven culture, taking time to pause can feel counterintuitive.
   - Solution: Remind yourself that mindfulness enhances productivity by improving focus and reducing stress.

Practical Mindfulness Exercises

1. **The Five Senses Exercise**
   Use your senses to ground yourself in the present moment:
   - Notice 5 things you can see.
   - Notice 4 things you can touch.
   - Notice 3 things you can hear.
   - Notice 2 things you can smell.
   - Notice 1 thing you can taste.
2. **Body Scan Meditation**
   Lie down or sit comfortably. Starting at your toes, slowly bring your attention to each part of your body, noticing any tension or sensations.
3. **Mindful Journaling**
   Spend 5–10 minutes writing about your thoughts and feelings without judgment. This helps you process emotions and gain clarity.

4. **Pause and Reflect**
   Set a reminder on your phone to pause for a minute every couple of hours. Use this time to take a deep breath and check in with yourself.

Action Steps to Incorporate Mindfulness into Your Life

1. **Start Small**
   Dedicate just one minute a day to mindfulness, gradually increasing as you feel comfortable.
2. **Create Mindful Habits**
   Pair mindfulness with daily activities, like brushing your teeth, drinking tea, or walking to the bus stop.
3. **Join a Mindfulness Group**
   Explore local mindfulness classes or online communities to learn and share experiences.
4. **Commit to a Mindfulness Challenge**
   Challenge yourself to practise mindfulness every day for a week. Reflect on the changes you notice in your mood, focus, and stress levels.

Conclusion: Mindfulness as a Path to Success

Mindfulness isn't just a tool for relaxation—it's a way of living that enhances every aspect of your life. By staying present, you can approach challenges with clarity, strengthen your relationships, and find joy in the simplest moments.

As you continue your journey to think and act like a winner, remember mindfulness is about progress, not perfection. Embrace it as a practice, and you'll discover a calmer, more focused version of yourself.

In the next chapter, we'll explore how winners embrace gratitude and generosity to amplify their success and positively impact the world around them. But for now, take a deep breath, pause, and reflect on this: How can mindfulness help you create space for success in your life today?

Success begins with awareness—start your journey now.

Chapter 18: Generosity – Giving Back to Amplify Success

Generosity isn't just about giving money—it's about sharing your time, energy, knowledge, and kindness to make a difference. Winners understand that true success isn't measured solely by personal achievements but by the impact they have on others. Generosity creates a ripple effect, strengthening relationships, building communities, and leaving a lasting legacy.

In the UK, generosity is woven into the fabric of society, from community fundraising events to nationwide campaigns like Children in Need. Whether it's supporting a local food bank or mentoring someone in your field, giving back is a powerful way to enrich your own life while uplifting others. This chapter explores how winners embrace generosity to create meaningful change.

Why Generosity Matters

"No one has ever become poor by giving." – Anne Frank

Generosity fosters connection, gratitude, and purpose. It helps you build stronger relationships, develop a sense of fulfilment, and contribute to a better world. Research even shows that acts of generosity release oxytocin and endorphins, boosting happiness and well-being.

Ask yourself: How often do you make time to give back? Generosity doesn't require grand gestures—small, thoughtful actions can create a big impact.

The Benefits of Generosity

1. **Strengthened Relationships**
   Generosity builds trust and goodwill, deepening your connections with others.
   - Example: Helping a neighbour with their shopping or offering to babysit for a friend strengthens your community ties.
2. **Personal Fulfilment**
   Helping others gives your life a sense of purpose and meaning.
   - Example: Volunteering at a local charity shop can be as rewarding for you as it is for the community you're helping.

3. **Professional Growth**
   Generosity in the workplace fosters collaboration, mentorship, and a positive reputation.
   - Example: Sharing your expertise with a junior colleague can help them grow while enhancing your leadership skills.
4. **Increased Resilience**
   Acts of giving remind you of your strengths and resources, helping you stay grounded during challenging times.
   - Tip: In moments of difficulty, consider what you can offer others—it often helps shift your focus from problems to possibilities.

How Winners Embrace Generosity

1. **Give Time**
   Time is one of the most valuable resources you can share.
   - Example: Dedicate a few hours a month to volunteering at a local shelter, tutoring students, or participating in community clean-ups.
2. **Share Knowledge**
   Mentoring or teaching others allows you to pass on valuable skills and insights.

- Example: Offer career advice to young professionals through initiatives like the Prince's Trust or your local university alumni network.

3. **Support Causes You Care About**
   Align your generosity with your passions to create the most meaningful impact.
   - Example: If you're passionate about wildlife conservation, consider donating to organisations like the RSPB or volunteering for beach clean-ups.

4. **Practice Everyday Acts of Kindness**
   Small, thoughtful gestures can brighten someone's day.
   - Example: Pay for someone's coffee, leave a kind note for a colleague, or offer a listening ear to a friend in need.

Generosity in the UK: Cultural Traditions

1. **Charity Events and Campaigns**
   The UK is known for its fundraising traditions, from bake sales and charity runs to national campaigns like Comic Relief and Macmillan Coffee Mornings.

- Tip: Get involved in local or national events to support causes you care about while connecting with others.
2. **Community Spirit**
   British communities often come together during times of need, whether it's organising food drives, helping during floods, or supporting NHS initiatives.
   - Example: Joining a local community group can be a great way to give back while fostering a sense of belonging.

Case Study: Marcus Rashford – A Champion of Generosity

Footballer Marcus Rashford exemplifies the power of generosity. Beyond his success on the pitch, Rashford has used his platform to campaign against child food poverty in the UK, successfully influencing government policies to provide free school meals during holidays.

His generosity extends beyond financial contributions—he has also shared his story to inspire others and mobilised communities to take action. Rashford's efforts demonstrate that generosity can drive meaningful change on both a local and national scale.

Overcoming Barriers to Generosity

1. **I Don't Have Enough Time**
   Many people feel they're too busy to give back.
   - Solution: Start small. Even 10 minutes a week can make a difference, whether it's checking in on a friend or donating online.
2. **I Don't Have Enough Money**
   Generosity doesn't require wealth.
   - Solution: Focus on non-monetary ways to give, such as volunteering, mentoring, or sharing resources.
3. **I Don't Know Where to Start**
   It can be overwhelming to choose a cause or figure out how to contribute.
   - Solution: Reflect on your passions and values, and start with something local or familiar, such as supporting a nearby charity or helping a friend in need.

Practical Ways to Practice Generosity in the UK

1. **Join a Local Charity**
   Many charities across the UK welcome volunteers for a variety of roles.

- Example: Organisations like Shelter, Age UK, and the Trussell Trust offer opportunities to get involved.
2. **Support Small Businesses**
Shopping locally and recommending small businesses to others supports your community.
    - Example: Leave positive reviews for your favourite café or shop on platforms like Google or TripAdvisor.
3. **Be an Active Listener**
Sometimes, generosity is as simple as giving someone your undivided attention.
    - Example: If a friend or colleague is struggling, offer to listen without judgment or interruption.
4. **Contribute to Crowdfunding Campaigns**
Platforms like JustGiving and GoFundMe make it easy to support causes and individuals in need.
    - Tip: Choose campaigns that align with your values or focus on your local community.

Generosity in the Workplace

1. **Mentor Colleagues**
   Share your skills and knowledge to help others grow.
   - Example: Offer to guide a new team member or provide constructive feedback on a project.
2. **Celebrate Others' Successes**
   Acknowledging achievements fosters a positive work environment.
   - Example: Send a congratulatory email or give a shout-out during a team meeting.
3. **Support Office Charity Initiatives**
   Many UK workplaces organise charity events like bake sales, fun runs, or dress-down days. Get involved to show your support.

Action Steps to Embrace Generosity Today

1. **Identify a Cause**
   Reflect on what you're passionate about and find ways to contribute, whether it's through time, money, or skills.

2. **Start Small**
   Commit to one act of generosity this week, such as donating to a food bank or writing a thank-you note to someone who's helped you.
3. **Get Involved Locally**
   Research community groups, charities, or initiatives in your area where you can make a difference.
4. **Incorporate Generosity into Your Routine**
   Make giving back a regular part of your life, such as volunteering monthly or setting aside a percentage of your income for charitable donations.

Conclusion: Generosity is the Gift That Keeps Giving

Generosity isn't just about helping others—it's about creating a life of purpose, connection, and fulfilment. By giving back, you enrich your own life while making a meaningful impact on the world around you.

As you continue your journey to think and act like a winner, remember success is amplified when it's shared. The more you give, the more you grow.

In the next chapter, we'll explore how winners cultivate courage to take risks, overcome fears, and seize opportunities. But for now, reflect on this: What's one act of generosity you can take today to make a difference in someone's life?

Generosity isn't just an action—it's a way of being. Start small and watch the ripple effects grow.

Chapter 19: Courage – Taking Risks and Seizing Opportunities

Courage is the willingness to step out of your comfort zone and face uncertainty, challenges, and fears. It's the driving force behind every bold decision and every meaningful achievement. Winners understand that without courage, growth is impossible. They embrace risks, learn from setbacks, and seize opportunities that others shy away from.

In the UK, courage is a trait deeply rooted in history and culture, from the bravery of suffragettes fighting for women's rights to the innovation of entrepreneurs like Sir Richard Branson. This chapter explores how winners cultivate courage to overcome obstacles, take risks, and achieve greatness.

Why Courage Matters

"Courage is not the absence of fear, but the triumph over it." – Nelson Mandela

Courage isn't about being fearless—it's about acting despite your fears. It allows you to face challenges head-on, make bold decisions, and step into the unknown with confidence.

Without courage, opportunities remain out of reach, and potential goes unfulfilled.

Ask yourself: What risks have you avoided because of fear? How might your life change if you approached challenges with courage instead?

The Different Types of Courage

1. **Physical Courage**
   This involves facing physical challenges or risks, whether in sports, professions, or daily life.
   - Example: Emergency responders in the UK, such as firefighters or paramedics, demonstrate physical courage every day.
2. **Emotional Courage**
   Facing difficult emotions or being vulnerable requires emotional bravery.
   - Example: Having an honest conversation with a loved one about a sensitive topic takes emotional courage.
3. **Moral Courage**
   Standing up for what's right, even when it's unpopular, reflects moral strength.

- Example: Activists in the UK, like those campaigning for climate change action, exhibit moral courage by advocating for important causes.

4. **Intellectual Courage**
   Challenging assumptions, embracing new ideas, and admitting when you're wrong require intellectual bravery.
   - Example: Being open to learning new skills or changing your perspective on an issue demonstrates intellectual courage.

How Winners Cultivate Courage

1. **Start Small**
   Courage grows through practice. Begin with small acts of bravery to build your confidence.
   - Example: Speak up in a meeting or try a new activity that pushes you slightly out of your comfort zone.
2. **Reframe Failure**
   Winners view failure as a stepping stone to success. Instead of fearing mistakes, they see them as opportunities to learn and grow.

- Tip: Keep a journal of lessons learned from past failures to remind yourself of how much you've grown.

3. **Visualise Success**
Use visualisation techniques to imagine yourself succeeding in a challenging situation.
    - Example: Before a presentation, picture yourself speaking confidently and receiving positive feedback.

4. **Seek Support**
Surround yourself with people who encourage and inspire you. Having a strong support system makes it easier to take risks.
    - Example: Join a professional network or community group to connect with like-minded individuals in the UK.

5. **Focus on Your "Why"**
A clear sense of purpose gives you the strength to act courageously.
    - Example: If your goal is to start a business, remind yourself why it's important—whether it's financial independence, pursuing your passion, or creating opportunities for others.

Taking Risks in the UK: A Cultural Perspective

1. **Calculated Risks in Business**
   The UK is home to many entrepreneurs who have taken bold risks to achieve success.
   - Example: Sir James Dyson took a risk by investing years in developing his first bagless vacuum cleaner, despite facing numerous rejections.
2. **Everyday Risks**
   Courage isn't limited to big decisions—it's also about taking everyday risks, such as starting a new hobby, applying for a promotion, or speaking up in a group setting.
   - Tip: Identify one small risk you can take this week to challenge yourself.
3. **Cultural Shifts**
   In the UK, where modesty and tradition often guide decision-making, embracing courage means balancing calculated risks with cultural norms.
   - Example: Advocating for change in a traditional workplace may require persistence and tact, but it can lead to meaningful progress.

Case Study: The Wright Sisters of Birmingham – Courage in the Face of Adversity

In the late 19th century, Annie and Jessie Wright became two of the first women to run a successful chain of tea shops in Birmingham, defying societal expectations and gender norms of the time.

Their courage to challenge traditional roles, innovate within the hospitality industry, and pursue their entrepreneurial dreams not only paved the way for other women but also left a lasting impact on their community.

Their story highlights the importance of courage in breaking barriers and seizing opportunities.

Overcoming Fear

Fear is often the biggest obstacle to courage. Winners overcome fear by:

1. **Acknowledging It**
   Pretending fear doesn't exist only gives it more power. Recognise your fears and face them head-on.
   - Tip: Write down your fears and explore why they exist. This helps you demystify and reduce their power.

2. **Breaking It Down**
   Large, intimidating challenges can be made more manageable by breaking them into smaller steps.
   - Example: If public speaking scares you, start by practising in front of a trusted friend before addressing a larger audience.
3. **Focusing on the Outcome**
   Remind yourself of the rewards of acting courageously.
   - Example: Applying for a challenging job may feel intimidating, but the potential for career growth makes the risk worthwhile.
4. **Practising Gratitude**
   Gratitude shifts your focus from fear to appreciation, creating a more positive mindset.
   - Tip: Reflect on past risks you've taken and how they've benefited you.

Practical Steps to Build Courage in Your Life

1. **Take One Small Risk Every Day**
   Consistently pushing your boundaries builds courage over time.

- Example: Try something new each day, like striking up a conversation with a stranger or exploring a different route on your commute.

2. **Challenge Limiting Beliefs**
Replace thoughts like "I can't do this" with empowering affirmations such as "I'm capable of learning and growing."

3. **Learn from Role Models**
Study the lives of courageous individuals, from historical figures to modern leaders, and draw inspiration from their stories.
   - Example: Read about the suffragettes who fought for women's rights in the UK.

4. **Celebrate Your Wins**
Acknowledge and reward yourself for every act of courage, no matter how small.
   - Example: Treat yourself after completing a difficult task or facing a fear.

Conclusion: Courage Unlocks Potential

Courage is the foundation of growth and achievement. It empowers you to overcome fear, take risks, and seize opportunities that lead to personal and professional success.

Whether you're advocating for change, pursuing a dream, or simply stepping out of your comfort zone, courage is the key to unlocking your potential.

As you continue your journey to think and act like a winner, remember courage isn't about being fearless—it's about taking action despite your fears.

In the next chapter, we'll explore how winners cultivate optimism to maintain a positive outlook and inspire those around them. But for now, reflect on this: What's one courageous step you can take today to move closer to your goals?

Bravery begins with a single act—take yours now.

Chapter 20: Optimism – Cultivating a Positive Mindset for Success

Optimism is more than just seeing the glass as half full—it's a mindset that helps you navigate challenges, seize opportunities, and inspire those around you. Winners understand that optimism isn't about ignoring difficulties; it's about focusing on possibilities and maintaining hope in the face of uncertainty.

In the UK, where discussions about the weather often lean toward the gloomy, cultivating optimism can be a powerful antidote to negativity. From navigating personal struggles to tackling professional challenges, optimism enables you to approach life with resilience, creativity, and confidence. This chapter explores how winners cultivate and sustain a positive outlook, no matter the circumstances.

Why Optimism Matters

"Pessimism leads to weakness, optimism to power." – William James

Optimism fuels motivation, strengthens relationships, and enhances problem-solving skills. It's not about blind positivity but about choosing to focus on solutions rather than obstacles.

Studies show that optimistic people are more likely to achieve their goals, experience better mental health, and build stronger networks.

Ask yourself: How do you react to setbacks? Do you dwell on the negatives, or do you seek out opportunities for growth? Optimism is a skill you can develop, and it starts with shifting your perspective.

The Science of Optimism

Optimism has tangible benefits for your brain and body. Research shows that a positive outlook:

1. Reduces stress by encouraging proactive problem-solving.
2. Boosts immunity, helping you stay healthier.
3. Improves cardiovascular health by reducing the impact of stress.

Cultivating optimism rewires your brain to focus on the positives, making it easier to handle challenges and achieve your goals.

Optimism in the UK: Everyday Positivity

1. **Finding Joy in Small Moments**
   British culture often celebrates the small pleasures in life—a walk in the countryside, a well-made cup of tea, or a good laugh with friends.
   - Tip: Pause to appreciate these moments and recognise the positivity they bring to your day.
2. **Turning Challenges into Opportunities**
   The UK's history is filled with examples of resilience and optimism, from rebuilding after WWII to adapting to modern challenges like Brexit and climate change.
   - Example: Approach changes in your own life with a similar mindset, focusing on opportunities rather than losses.

How Winners Cultivate Optimism

1. **Reframe Negative Thoughts**
   Optimists challenge negative thoughts and replace them with empowering alternatives.
   - Example: Instead of thinking, "I'll never get this promotion," reframe it as, "I'll focus on improving my skills and showcasing my value."

2. **Focus on What You Can Control**
   Winners don't dwell on things outside their control. They focus their energy on actions that can make a difference.
   - Example: If your train is delayed, use the time to catch up on reading or plan your day rather than stressing about the delay.
3. **Surround Yourself with Positive Influences**
   Optimism is contagious. Surrounding yourself with positive, supportive people helps you maintain a constructive mindset.
   - Example: Join local groups or online communities in the UK that focus on personal development or shared interests.
4. **Practice Gratitude**
   Focusing on what you're thankful for shifts your perspective from scarcity to abundance.
   - Tip: Keep a gratitude journal and write down three things you're grateful for each day.

Case Study: Captain Sir Tom Moore – A Beacon of Optimism

Captain Sir Tom Moore captured the hearts of the UK during the COVID-19 pandemic with his fundraising efforts for the NHS. At 99 years old, he walked 100 laps in his garden, raising over £32 million and inspiring millions with his message: "Tomorrow will be a good day."

His optimism and determination turned a simple idea into a national movement, demonstrating the power of positivity to unite and uplift.

Overcoming Barriers to Optimism

1. **Negative Environments**
   Being surrounded by negativity can make it harder to stay optimistic.
   - Solution: Limit exposure to negative influences and seek out uplifting content, such as inspirational books or podcasts.
2. **Fear of Disappointment**
   Some people avoid optimism to protect themselves from potential disappointment.
   - Solution: Remember that optimism isn't about ignoring risks—it's about believing in your ability to handle them.

3. **Setbacks and Failures**
   Challenges can shake your confidence and make it difficult to stay positive.
   - Solution: Reflect on past successes and remind yourself that setbacks are temporary and part of the journey.

Practical Ways to Cultivate Optimism in the UK

1. **Embrace Nature**
   Spending time in nature is proven to boost mood and perspective.
   - Tip: Take a walk in the Lake District, along the Jurassic Coast, or in your local park to reconnect with the natural world.
2. **Celebrate Small Wins**
   Recognising small achievements builds momentum and reinforces positivity.
   - Example: Treat yourself to a favourite meal after completing a challenging project.
3. **Use Positive Language**
   The words you use shape your mindset. Choose language that reflects hope and possibility.
   - Example: Replace "I can't" with "I'm working on it" or "I'll try."

4. **Volunteer or Give Back**
   Helping others fosters a sense of purpose and gratitude, which fuels optimism.
   - Example: Volunteer at a local food bank or participate in a community clean-up initiative.

Action Steps to Build Optimism

1. **Start Your Day with Positivity**
   Begin each morning by reflecting on something you're looking forward to or grateful for.
2. **Reframe Setbacks**
   The next time you face a challenge, ask yourself: What's the lesson here? How can I grow from this?
3. **Surround Yourself with Positivity**
   Spend time with people who inspire and uplift you. Avoid excessive exposure to negative news or gossip.
4. **Create a Positivity Ritual**
   Dedicate time each day to something that brings you joy, whether it's listening to music, reading, or spending time outdoors.

Conclusion: Optimism is a Choice

Optimism isn't about ignoring life's difficulties—it's about facing them with hope, resilience, and a belief in your ability to overcome them. By cultivating a positive mindset, you can approach challenges with confidence, inspire those around you, and unlock new opportunities for growth and success.

As you continue your journey to think and act like a winner, remember optimism is a habit you can build, one thought and one action at a time.

In the next chapter, we'll explore how winners master decision-making to take bold, decisive actions and achieve their goals. But for now, reflect on this: What's one way you can practise optimism today?

Positivity transforms lives—start with your own.

Chapter 21: Decision-Making – Taking Bold, Decisive Actions

Decisions shape our lives. From small, everyday choices to life-changing decisions, the ability to make bold and informed choices is what sets winners apart. They understand that indecision is the enemy of progress and that taking action—no matter how uncertain the outcome—moves them closer to their goals.

In the UK, where traditional values often emphasise caution and deliberation, mastering the art of decision-making involves balancing careful thought with the courage to act. Whether it's a career move, a financial decision, or a personal choice, learning how to decide effectively and confidently is a skill that can transform your life.

This chapter explores how winners approach decision-making, overcome doubt, and make choices that lead to success.

Why Decision-Making Matters

"Once you make a decision, the universe conspires to make it happen." – Ralph Waldo Emerson

Every decision, big or small, shapes the trajectory of your life. While some choices may seem insignificant at the time, they often set the stage for bigger opportunities. Winners recognise the power of decisions and approach them with clarity, confidence, and purpose.

Ask yourself: How do you make decisions? Are you deliberate and confident, or do you procrastinate and second-guess yourself? Effective decision-making is a skill that can be developed with practice and intention.

The Challenges of Decision-Making

1. **Fear of Failure**
   The fear of making the wrong choice can lead to indecision or avoidance.
   - Example: Hesitating to apply for a new job because you're unsure if it's the right fit.
2. **Overthinking**
   Spending too much time analysing options can lead to paralysis by analysis.
   - Example: Deliberating endlessly over which savings account to open, rather than choosing one and getting started.

3. **External Pressure**
   Decisions can be influenced by societal expectations, family opinions, or peer pressure.
   - Example: Choosing a career path based on what others expect rather than what you truly want.
4. **Lack of Clarity**
   Unclear goals or priorities make it difficult to evaluate your options.
   - Example: Struggling to decide between moving to a new city or staying put because you haven't defined your long-term goals.

How Winners Approach Decision-Making

1. **Clarify Your Goals**
   Winners make decisions based on their values and objectives. When you know what you're working toward, the right choices become clearer.
   - Example: If your goal is financial independence, decisions about spending, saving, and investing become easier to navigate.

2. **Gather Information, but Don't Overload**
   Winners strike a balance between gathering enough information to make an informed choice and avoiding overanalyses.
   - Tip: Set a time limit for research to prevent endless deliberation.
3. **Trust Your Instincts**
   Intuition often plays a key role in decision-making. Trusting your gut, especially when combined with logical reasoning, can lead to confident choices.
   - Example: Many successful entrepreneurs in the UK, like Deborah Meaden, credit their instincts for guiding their business decisions.
4. **Evaluate the Risks and Rewards**
   Winners assess the potential risks and benefits of each option, weighing them against their goals and values.
   - Example: Before starting a business, consider factors like financial investment, time commitment, and potential long-term rewards.
5. **Take Action**
   Decisiveness is key. Winners understand that no decision is perfect, but taking action is better than remaining stagnant.

- Tip: Break big decisions into smaller, actionable steps to make them less overwhelming.

The Power of Decisiveness

In the UK's fast-paced business environment, decisiveness is often what separates leaders from followers. Whether you're making a split-second call in a crisis or planning a long-term strategy, the ability to act confidently inspires trust and drives progress.

1. **Decisiveness Builds Momentum**
   Taking action creates momentum, which leads to more opportunities and growth.
   - Example: Accepting a new project at work may lead to skill development, promotions, or networking opportunities.
2. **Decisiveness Reduces Anxiety**
   Prolonged indecision can create stress and uncertainty. Making a choice, even if it's not perfect, provides clarity and direction.

Case Study: Winston Churchill's Leadership Decisions

Winston Churchill, one of the UK's most iconic leaders, faced countless critical decisions during his tenure as Prime Minister. His ability to make bold, decisive choices, such as leading Britain through World War II with strategic military and political moves, showcases the importance of confidence and clarity in decision-making.

Churchill's leadership reminds us that even in the face of uncertainty, the willingness to decide and act can lead to extraordinary outcomes.

Practical Decision-Making Frameworks

1. **The 10-10-10 Rule**
   Ask yourself: How will this decision impact me in 10 minutes, 10 months, and 10 years?
   - Example: If you're considering buying a new car, think about the immediate financial impact, how it will affect your budget in the coming year, and whether it aligns with your long-term financial goals.

2. **The Eisenhower Matrix**
   Organise decisions based on urgency and importance:
   - Urgent and important: Do it now.
   - Important but not urgent: Schedule it.
   - Urgent but not important: Delegate it.
   - Neither urgent nor important: Eliminate it.
3. **Pros and Cons List**
   A simple but effective tool to weigh the advantages and disadvantages of each option.
   - Example: Use this approach when deciding whether to relocate for a job opportunity.
4. **SWOT Analysis**
   Evaluate the Strengths, Weaknesses, Opportunities, and Threats of each option to make an informed choice.

Overcoming Fear of Failure

1. **Reframe Failure**
   Winners see failure as feedback. Every decision, whether it leads to success or not, is an opportunity to learn.

- Example: If a career move doesn't work out, focus on the skills and experience you gained from the role.
2. **Focus on the Process, Not Just the Outcome**
   Good decisions don't always lead to perfect outcomes, but they build your decision-making skills over time.
3. **Set a Deadline**
   Giving yourself a clear timeframe to decide reduces the risk of overthinking.

Action Steps to Improve Decision-Making

1. **Define Your Priorities**
   Write down your top three personal and professional goals. Use these as a guide for evaluating decisions.
2. **Simplify Small Decisions**
   Streamline routine choices, like what to wear or eat, to save mental energy for bigger decisions.
3. **Seek Advice**
   Talk to mentors, colleagues, or trusted friends for perspective, but remember that the final decision is yours.

4. **Reflect and Learn**
   After making a decision, reflect on the outcome and what you can learn for next time.

Conclusion: Decisions Shape Your Destiny

Every decision you make is a step toward shaping the life you want. Winners don't wait for certainty—they embrace the unknown, trust their instincts, and take bold action. By developing confidence in your decision-making process, you can navigate challenges, seize opportunities, and move closer to your goals.

As you continue your journey to think and act like a winner, remember indecision is a choice to stand still. Start small, build momentum, and watch your decisions transform your life.

In the next chapter, we'll explore how winners build lasting relationships that support and enhance their journey to success. But for now, reflect on this: What decision have you been avoiding, and how can you take the first step today?

Decide to act—the rest will follow.

Chapter 22: Building Relationships – The Foundation of Long-Term Success

No one achieves success alone. Relationships are the cornerstone of a fulfilling and impactful life, whether they're personal, professional, or community-based. Winners understand that meaningful connections open doors, provide support, and create opportunities for growth. They prioritise building and nurturing relationships, knowing that the quality of their network often determines the quality of their life.

In the UK, where the tradition of community and collaboration runs deep—from the close-knit camaraderie of local pubs to the teamwork of professional environments—relationships play a vital role in achieving long-term success. This chapter explores how winners build, maintain, and strengthen relationships that elevate their lives and the lives of others.

Why Relationships Matter

"Success is not just about what you know, but who you know." – Unknown

Relationships provide support, inspiration, and opportunities. They help you weather challenges, celebrate achievements, and expand your horizons. The people you surround yourself with shape your mindset, influence your decisions, and help you grow.

Ask yourself: Are you investing enough in your relationships? Do you actively seek to build meaningful connections, or are you letting them happen by chance?

The Benefits of Strong Relationships

1. **Emotional Support**
   Close relationships provide comfort and encouragement during difficult times.
   - Example: Having a trusted friend or partner to talk to during a career change can ease stress and provide clarity.
2. **Career Advancement**
   Networking opens doors to new opportunities and insights.
   - Example: In the UK's professional landscape, joining organisations like the Chartered Institute of Management can connect you with mentors and industry leaders.

3. **Increased Happiness**
   Studies show that strong relationships are one of the most significant predictors of happiness and life satisfaction.
   - Example: Sharing a meal with friends or spending quality time with family can boost your mood and strengthen your bonds.
4. **Collaboration and Growth**
   Working with others enhances creativity and problem-solving.
   - Example: Joining a local startup community or business group can spark innovative ideas and partnerships.

How Winners Build Meaningful Relationships

1. **Be Genuine**
   Authenticity is the foundation of trust and connection. Winners approach relationships with honesty and sincerity, focusing on mutual respect and shared values.
   - Tip: Be yourself, and let others see your strengths and vulnerabilities.

2. **Listen Actively**
   Great relationships start with great communication. Winners listen more than they speak, showing genuine interest in others' thoughts and feelings.
   - Example: During conversations, put your phone away and focus entirely on the person you're speaking with.
3. **Offer Value**
   Relationships thrive when both parties contribute. Winners look for ways to help, support, or uplift others without expecting anything in return.
   - Example: Share resources, introduce contacts, or offer advice when you can.
4. **Invest Time and Energy**
   Building relationships requires consistent effort. Winners prioritise spending time with the people who matter most.
   - Tip: Schedule regular catch-ups with friends, family, or colleagues, whether it's a coffee, a walk, or a video call.

Building Professional Relationships in the UK

1. **Network Strategically**
   Attend industry events, seminars, and workshops to meet like-minded professionals.
   - Example: In the UK, events like the London Business Show or Tech Week provide excellent networking opportunities.
2. **Join Professional Organisations**
   Membership in organisations like the Chartered Institute of Marketing or the Institute of Directors can connect you with peers and mentors.
3. **Use LinkedIn Effectively**
   LinkedIn is a powerful tool for connecting with professionals in the UK and beyond.
   - Tip: Personalise your connection requests and engage with your network by commenting on posts or sharing valuable content.

Nurturing Personal Relationships

1. **Be Present**
   Quality time is more important than quantity. Winners prioritise being fully present with loved ones.

- Example: Turn off distractions during family dinners or outings and focus on meaningful conversations.

2. **Express Gratitude**
Regularly showing appreciation strengthens bonds.
    - Example: Write a thank-you note to a friend who has supported you or surprise a loved one with a thoughtful gesture.

3. **Resolve Conflicts Constructively**
Disagreements are natural, but how you handle them matters. Winners address issues with empathy and a focus on finding solutions.
    - Tip: Use "I" statements to express your feelings without blaming the other person (e.g., "I feel hurt when...").

Case Study: The Power of Networking – Richard Branson

Sir Richard Branson, founder of the Virgin Group, is known not only for his entrepreneurial success but also for his exceptional ability to build relationships. Branson attributes much of his success to his network, emphasising the importance of listening, valuing others' contributions, and fostering collaboration.

Branson's approach demonstrates that relationships are not just a tool for success—they're a cornerstone of sustainable growth and innovation.

Challenges in Building Relationships and How to Overcome Them

1. **Lack of Time**
   Busy schedules can make it hard to prioritise relationships.
   - Solution: Treat relationships like any other important commitment—schedule time for them and stick to it.

2. **Fear of Rejection**
   The fear of being judged or turned down can hold you back from reaching out.
   - Solution: Remember that most people are open to connection and appreciate genuine interest. Take small steps, like starting a conversation or sending a friendly message.
3. **Maintaining Long-Distance Relationships**
   Physical distance can strain connections.
   - Solution: Use technology like video calls or messaging apps to stay in touch and plan visits whenever possible.

Practical Ways to Build and Strengthen Relationships in the UK

1. **Host Gatherings**
   Organise casual meetups, like a dinner party or a picnic in a local park, to bring people together.
   - Example: Invite friends or colleagues for a Sunday roast or a pub quiz night.

2. **Volunteer Together**
   Joining community initiatives or charity events allows you to bond while giving back.
   - Example: Participate in a litter-picking event or volunteer at a food bank with friends or family.

3. **Join Clubs or Groups**
   Being part of a group with shared interests is a great way to meet people and deepen relationships.
   - **Example:** Join a local sports club, a book group, or even a hobbyist society like photography or gardening. Organisations such as Meetup.com or your local council's community page can help you find groups near you.

4. **Celebrate Milestones**
   Acknowledging birthdays, anniversaries, or achievements strengthens bonds and shows you care.
   - **Tip:** Send a handwritten card or plan a small celebration to make the occasion memorable.

5. **Participate in British Traditions**
   Engage in cultural or seasonal traditions to bond with those around you.
   - **Example:** Host a Bonfire Night gathering, join a village fete, or attend a Christmas market with friends and family.

Building Online Relationships

1. **Engage with Online Communities**
   Social media and online forums can connect you with people who share your passions or professional interests.
   - **Example:** Join groups on Facebook or Reddit focused on topics like UK hiking trails, financial planning, or parenting.
2. **Be Thoughtful in Digital Communication**
   Whether through email, messaging, or social media, ensure your interactions are positive and engaging.
   - **Tip:** Share useful articles, respond with meaningful comments, and avoid overly generic messages.
3. **Organise Virtual Meetups**
   For long-distance friends or professional contacts, hosting a virtual coffee or quiz night can keep connections alive.

- **Example:** Use Zoom or Microsoft Teams to stay connected with colleagues or distant friends.

Action Steps to Build Stronger Relationships

1. **Reconnect with Someone**
   Reach out to an old friend or colleague you haven't spoken to in a while. A simple message or call can rekindle the connection.
2. **Make Time for One-on-One Interactions**
   Focus on spending quality time with someone important to you this week, whether it's a partner, parent, or mentor.
3. **Attend a Networking Event**
   Look for opportunities to meet new people in your industry or community. Check platforms like Eventbrite or LinkedIn for events near you.
4. **Be a Giver, Not Just a Taker**
   Offer help, advice, or support without expecting anything in return. Generosity strengthens trust and rapport.

Conclusion: Relationships Are the Foundation of Success

Success isn't just about what you achieve—it's about who you share it with. Strong relationships provide the support, inspiration, and opportunities you need to thrive.

Whether it's connecting with a trusted mentor, nurturing a close friendship, or building a professional network, investing in relationships is one of the most rewarding things you can do.

As you continue your journey to think and act like a winner, remember relationships are not a byproduct of success—they're a driving force behind it.

In the next chapter, we'll explore how Resilience is formed by turning setbacks into stepping stones.

Great connections lead to great opportunities— start building them today.

Chapter 23: Resilience – Turning Setbacks into Stepping Stones

Resilience is the ability to bounce back from adversity, adapt to challenges, and keep moving forward. It's what separates those who give up in the face of setbacks from those who rise stronger. Winners understand that failure is not the end but a stepping stone to success. Resilience helps them stay focused, motivated, and optimistic, even in the most trying times.

In the UK, where resilience has been a hallmark of history—from enduring the Blitz during WWII to navigating modern challenges like Brexit and the pandemic—this trait is deeply valued. Whether it's rebuilding after personal loss or persevering in a competitive career, resilience empowers you to overcome obstacles and achieve your goals.

This chapter explores how winners cultivate resilience, learn from failure, and thrive under pressure.

Why Resilience Matters

"Success is not final; failure is not fatal: It is the courage to continue that counts." – Winston Churchill

Life is full of ups and downs. Resilience allows you to navigate uncertainty, learn from setbacks, and keep striving for success. It's not about avoiding difficulties but about developing the strength to face them head-on.

Ask yourself: How do you handle setbacks? Do you view them as insurmountable roadblocks or opportunities to grow? Resilience begins with a mindset shift—seeing challenges as part of the journey rather than the end of it.

The Science of Resilience

Resilience isn't a fixed trait—it's a skill you can develop. Research shows that resilience is linked to:

1. **Mental Flexibility:** The ability to adapt to changing circumstances.
2. **Emotional Regulation:** Managing stress and emotions effectively.
3. **Social Support:** Building strong relationships that provide encouragement and perspective.

By developing these traits, you can strengthen your ability to handle adversity and thrive in difficult situations.

Building Resilience in Everyday Life

1. **Reframe Challenges**
   Winners see setbacks as opportunities to learn and grow.
   - Example: If you didn't get a promotion, view it as a chance to develop new skills or explore other opportunities.
2. **Focus on What You Can Control**
   Resilient individuals concentrate on the factors within their control, rather than worrying about things they can't change.
   - Tip: Make a list of actionable steps you can take to improve your situation, whether it's updating your CV or seeking feedback.
3. **Cultivate Optimism**
   Maintaining a positive outlook helps you stay motivated and focused during tough times.
   - Example: Instead of dwelling on a failure, remind yourself of past successes and the progress you've made.
4. **Build a Support Network**
   Strong relationships provide emotional support and practical advice when you're facing challenges.

- Tip: Reach out to friends, family, or mentors in the UK who can offer encouragement and guidance.

How Winners Cultivate Resilience

1. **Embrace Failure as Feedback**
   Winners don't fear failure—they use it as a learning tool.
   - Example: J.K. Rowling faced multiple rejections before publishing *Harry Potter*. Her resilience turned rejection into one of the greatest literary successes of all time.
2. **Practice Self-Care**
   Resilience requires physical and emotional energy. Winners prioritise rest, nutrition, and exercise to maintain their strength.
   - Tip: Take a walk in a local park or enjoy a traditional British Sunday roast with family to recharge.
3. **Set Realistic Goals**
   Breaking down big challenges into smaller, achievable steps makes them less overwhelming.
   - Example: If you're tackling debt, start by creating a budget or setting up a small monthly savings plan.

4. **Develop Problem-Solving Skills**
   Resilient individuals approach problems with a solutions-oriented mindset.
   - Tip: When faced with a challenge, brainstorm multiple solutions and weigh the pros and cons of each.

Resilience in UK History

The UK's history is filled with examples of resilience:

1. **The Blitz:** During WWII, Londoners endured nightly bombings with remarkable strength, often continuing their daily routines amidst the chaos.
2. **Post-Brexit Adaptations:** Businesses and individuals across the UK have shown resilience by adapting to new trade regulations and market conditions.
3. **The NHS:** Healthcare workers have demonstrated extraordinary resilience, especially during the COVID-19 pandemic, providing care under immense pressure.

These examples highlight how resilience enables individuals and communities to overcome adversity and emerge stronger.

Case Study: Dame Kelly Holmes – Resilience in Sport

Dame Kelly Holmes, one of Britain's greatest athletes, exemplifies resilience. Before winning double gold at the 2004 Athens Olympics, Holmes faced years of injuries and setbacks. Her ability to persevere, adapt her training, and maintain a positive mindset led to her ultimate success.

Holmes's story is a powerful reminder that resilience is often the key to achieving long-term goals, even when the journey is fraught with challenges.

Overcoming Barriers to Resilience

1. **Negative Self-Talk**
   Internal criticism can undermine your ability to bounce back.
   - Solution: Replace negative thoughts with empowering affirmations, such as, "I have the strength to overcome this challenge."
2. **Isolation**
   Facing adversity alone can make it harder to recover.
   - Solution: Reach out to friends, family, or support groups for encouragement and perspective.

3. **Burnout**
   Chronic stress can deplete your resilience over time.
   - Solution: Prioritise rest and self-care and set boundaries to avoid overcommitting.

Practical Steps to Build Resilience in the UK

1. **Engage in Community Activities**
   Joining local groups or volunteering can provide a sense of purpose and connection.
   - Example: Participate in initiatives like community gardening, charity runs, or neighbourhood clean-ups.
2. **Explore the Outdoors**
   Spending time in nature is proven to reduce stress and boost resilience.
   - Tip: Take a weekend trip to the Lake District, Snowdonia, or your nearest national park for a mental reset.
3. **Set Daily Intentions**
   Start each day by identifying one positive action you'll take, no matter how small.
   - Example: Commit to a morning walk, writing in a journal, or calling a friend.

4. **Celebrate Progress**
   Recognise and reward yourself for overcoming challenges, even if the steps feel small.
   - Example: Treat yourself to a favourite meal or activity after completing a difficult project.

Action Steps to Build Resilience Today

1. **Reflect on Past Challenges**
   Write down a time when you overcame adversity and the lessons you learned. Use this as a reminder of your strength.
2. **Identify Your Support System**
   List the people you can turn to for advice or encouragement. Make an effort to strengthen those connections.
3. **Adopt a Growth Mindset**
   Embrace challenges as opportunities to learn and grow, rather than as obstacles to avoid.
4. **Practice Gratitude**
   Focus on the positive aspects of your life, even during tough times. This helps shift your mindset from scarcity to abundance.

Conclusion: Resilience is the Key to Growth

Resilience is not about avoiding challenges—it's about rising stronger every time you fall. By cultivating a resilient mindset, you can navigate life's ups and downs with confidence and grace. Winners understand that setbacks are an inevitable part of the journey, but they use them as fuel to achieve even greater heights.

As you continue your journey to think and act like a winner, remember resilience isn't something you're born with—it's something you build through practice, reflection, and determination.

In the next chapter, we'll explore how winners cultivate discipline to stay consistent and focused on their goals. But for now, reflect on this: How can you turn your current challenges into stepping stones for success?

Resilience is your superpower—embrace it and keep moving forward.

Chapter 24: Discipline – Staying Consistent on the Path to Success

Discipline is the bridge between goals and achievements. It's the ability to stay consistent, focused, and committed, even when motivation wanes or challenges arise. Winners understand that success isn't about fleeting bursts of effort— it's about showing up every day and doing the work, no matter how they feel.

In the UK, where balancing work, family, and personal goals is often a juggling act, discipline is key to staying on track. From creating daily routines to building habits that align with long-term aspirations, discipline allows you to move steadily toward success without being derailed by distractions or setbacks. This chapter explores how winners cultivate discipline and use it to achieve extraordinary results.

Why Discipline Matters

"Discipline is the refining fire by which talent becomes ability." – Roy L. Smith

Discipline helps you overcome procrastination, push through challenges, and maintain progress toward your goals. It's not about perfection—it's about persistence. While motivation gets you started, discipline keeps you going.

Ask yourself: How disciplined are you in pursuing your goals? Do you stay consistent, or do you let distractions and excuses pull you off track? Discipline is a skill that anyone can develop with the right mindset and strategies.

The Key Principles of Discipline

1. **Consistency is Key**
   Small, daily actions lead to big results over time. Winners focus on building routines that support their goals.
   - **Example:** Committing to 30 minutes of exercise each day is more effective than sporadic bursts of intense activity.
2. **Delayed Gratification**
   Discipline requires prioritising long-term rewards over immediate pleasures.
   - **Example:** Saving for a deposit on a home in the UK requires forgoing some short-term luxuries like expensive holidays or dining out.

3. **Self-Control**
   The ability to resist temptations and stay focused on your priorities is essential.
   - **Example:** Avoiding distractions like social media during work hours helps you maintain productivity.

How Winners Cultivate Discipline

1. **Set Clear Goals**
   Discipline starts with knowing what you're working toward. Winners set specific, measurable, and realistic goals to guide their efforts.
   - **Example:** Instead of saying, "I want to get fit," set a goal like, "I'll run a 5K in 12 weeks by training three times a week."
2. **Create a Routine**
   Consistent routines make discipline easier by reducing decision fatigue.
   - **Example:** Establish a morning routine that includes planning your day, exercising, and reviewing your goals.
3. **Use Tools and Systems**
   Winners use tools to stay organised and accountable.

- Example: Use a planner or apps like Todoist or Trello to track your tasks and progress.
4. **Hold Yourself Accountable**
Regularly reviewing your progress helps you stay disciplined and adjust your approach as needed.
    - Tip: Share your goals with a friend or mentor who can provide support and accountability.
5. **Embrace Discomfort**
Winners know that growth often requires stepping outside their comfort zone.
    - Example: If public speaking makes you nervous, commit to practising regularly until you feel more confident.

Discipline in Everyday UK Life

1. **Managing Finances**
Discipline is essential for financial stability and growth, especially with the rising cost of living in the UK.
    - Example: Set up direct debits for savings and investments to ensure you're consistently building your financial future.

2. **Balancing Work and Life**
   Maintaining discipline in your schedule allows you to balance professional and personal commitments.
   - **Example:** Use your lunch break to recharge by taking a walk or reading, rather than scrolling through social media.
3. **Staying Active**
   The UK offers countless opportunities to build physical discipline, from joining a local gym to participating in community sports leagues.
   - **Example:** Sign up for parkrun, a free, weekly 5K event held across the UK, to stay consistent with your fitness goals.

Overcoming Challenges to Discipline

1. **Lack of Motivation**
   Motivation comes and goes, but discipline keeps you moving forward.
   - **Solution:** Focus on your "why" and remember the long-term benefits of your efforts.
2. **Procrastination**
   Putting things off can derail your progress.

- **Solution:** Use the two-minute rule: If a task takes less than two minutes, do it immediately.
3. **Burnout**
Overcommitting without rest can lead to exhaustion.
    - **Solution:** Build rest and recovery into your routine to maintain balance and avoid burnout.
4. **Distractions**
External interruptions can disrupt your focus.
    - **Solution:** Create a focused work environment by silencing notifications and setting clear boundaries.

Case Study: Sir Andy Murray – The Discipline of a Champion

Sir Andy Murray, one of Britain's most celebrated athletes, exemplifies the power of discipline. His commitment to rigorous training, mental preparation, and continuous improvement has earned him multiple Grand Slam titles and an Olympic gold medal.

Even when faced with injuries and setbacks, Murray's discipline kept him focused on recovery and returning to competition.

His story highlights how consistent effort and unwavering determination can overcome obstacles and lead to extraordinary success.

Practical Steps to Build Discipline

1. **Start Small**
   Focus on building one habit at a time to avoid feeling overwhelmed.
   - **Example:** Begin with a 10-minute daily walk before progressing to more intense exercise routines.
2. **Reward Yourself**
   Celebrating small milestones reinforces your efforts and keeps you motivated.
   - **Example:** Treat yourself to a night out or a favourite meal after hitting a monthly savings goal.
3. **Track Your Progress**
   Visualising your progress helps you stay motivated and disciplined.
   - **Tip:** Use a habit tracker or journal to record your achievements and reflect on your growth.

4. **Prepare for Setbacks**
   Anticipate challenges and plan how you'll address them.
   - **Example:** If you know you'll have a busy week at work, schedule shorter, more manageable workouts instead of skipping them altogether.

Discipline vs. Motivation

While motivation is important for getting started, it's discipline that sustains you over the long haul. Winners rely on discipline to keep moving forward, even on days when they don't feel motivated.

1. **Motivation is Emotional:** It's influenced by moods and external factors.
2. **Discipline is Logical:** It's a deliberate choice to act, regardless of how you feel.

Action Steps to Build Discipline Today

1. **Define Your Goals**
   Write down a specific goal and break it into actionable steps.
2. **Establish a Routine**
   Identify one habit that supports your goal and commit to practising it daily.

3. **Set Accountability**
   Share your goal with a trusted friend or join a community group for support.
4. **Reflect Regularly**
   At the end of each week, review your progress and adjust your approach if needed.

Conclusion: Discipline is the Key to Consistency

Discipline is the foundation of success. It helps you stay focused, push through challenges, and achieve your goals, one step at a time. By cultivating discipline, you create a life of structure, purpose, and progress.

As you continue your journey to think and act like a winner, remember discipline is a choice you make every day. Start small, stay consistent, and trust the process.

In the next chapter, we'll explore how winners use creativity and innovation to solve problems and stay ahead in a competitive world. But for now, reflect on this: What's one habit you can commit to today to strengthen your discipline?

Consistency leads to greatness—start your journey now.

Chapter 25: Creativity and Innovation – Staying Ahead in a Competitive World

Creativity and innovation are essential for success in today's fast-paced world. Whether it's solving complex problems, launching a new business, or finding fresh approaches to everyday challenges, the ability to think creatively sets winners apart. They understand that creativity isn't just for artists—it's a skill that can be cultivated and applied in any field.

In the UK, a hub of innovation and creativity—from Shakespeare's literary genius to the tech start-ups of Silicon Roundabout—embracing these traits has long been a cornerstone of progress. This chapter explores how winners harness creativity and innovation to stay ahead, adapt to change, and turn ideas into impactful realities.

Why Creativity and Innovation Matter

"The true sign of intelligence is not knowledge but imagination." – Albert Einstein

Creativity enables you to see possibilities where others see obstacles, while innovation turns those possibilities into tangible results. In a competitive world, these skills help you stand out, solve problems, and seize opportunities.

Ask yourself: How often do you challenge the status quo? Are you exploring new ideas or sticking to familiar routines? Cultivating creativity requires a willingness to experiment, take risks, and think differently.

The Difference Between Creativity and Innovation

1. **Creativity**
   The ability to generate original ideas or think in novel ways.
   - **Example:** Brainstorming a unique marketing campaign for a new product.
2. **Innovation**
   The process of turning creative ideas into practical solutions or products.
   - **Example:** Developing a prototype for a new piece of technology and bringing it to market.

Both are interdependent—creativity sparks the idea, and innovation brings it to life.

How Winners Foster Creativity

1. **Embrace Curiosity**
   Winners are curious about the world around them. They ask questions, seek new experiences, and explore diverse perspectives.
   - **Tip:** Visit museums, attend cultural events, or read books on topics outside your field to spark fresh ideas.
2. **Create Time for Reflection**
   Creativity thrives in moments of quiet and focus.
   - **Example:** Set aside time each week for brainstorming or journaling without distractions.
3. **Collaborate with Others**
   Great ideas often come from collaboration. Working with others exposes you to new viewpoints and approaches.
   - **Example:** Join a co-working space or professional organisation in the UK to connect with creative thinkers in your industry.
4. **Challenge Assumptions**
   Winners question conventional wisdom and explore alternative ways of thinking.

- **Tip:** Ask "What if?" questions to reimagine existing processes or solutions.

Innovation in the UK: A Culture of Creativity

1. **Historic Achievements**
   The UK has a long history of innovation, from the industrial revolution to modern breakthroughs like the creation of the World Wide Web by Sir Tim Berners-Lee.
2. **Thriving Creative Industries**
   The UK's creative industries—such as film, fashion, and design—are among the most influential in the world, contributing billions to the economy.
3. **Innovation Hubs**
   Areas like London's Silicon Roundabout and Manchester's MediaCityUK are hotbeds for start-ups and creative ventures, providing resources and networking opportunities for innovators.

How Winners Drive Innovation

1. **Take Risks**
   Innovation often involves stepping into the unknown. Winners are willing to take calculated risks to explore new possibilities.

- **Example:** Pitching an unconventional idea at work or launching a side project in your free time.
2. **Focus on Problem-Solving**
Innovation begins with identifying challenges and finding better solutions.
    - **Example:** Use customer feedback to refine a product or service, ensuring it meets real-world needs.
3. **Leverage Technology**
Staying ahead requires embracing technological advancements.
    - **Tip:** Explore tools like AI, automation, or data analytics to enhance your work or business.
4. **Stay Adaptable**
Winners remain open to change and pivot when necessary.
    - **Example:** During the COVID-19 pandemic, many UK businesses innovated by shifting to online operations or offering new services.

Case Study: Dyson – Innovation Through Design

Sir James Dyson revolutionised household appliances with his innovative vacuum cleaner designs. His journey wasn't without challenges — Dyson faced over 5,000 prototypes and countless rejections before launching his first product.

Today, Dyson is a global brand known for its creativity and commitment to solving problems through design and technology. This story highlights how persistence and a focus on innovation can turn a bold idea into a game-changing success.

Overcoming Barriers to Creativity and Innovation

1. **Fear of Failure**
   Worrying about mistakes can stifle creativity.
   - **Solution:** Reframe failure as an opportunity to learn and improve.
2. **Lack of Time**
   Busy schedules can leave little room for brainstorming or experimentation.
   - **Solution:** Block out dedicated time for creative thinking or problem-solving.

3. **Resistance to Change**
   Comfort with the status quo can hinder innovation.
   - **Solution:** Challenge yourself to try new approaches, even if they feel uncomfortable at first.

Practical Steps to Boost Creativity and Innovation in the UK

1. **Engage in Creative Activities**
   Hobbies like painting, writing, or playing music can enhance your ability to think creatively.
   - **Example:** Attend a local art workshop or join a choir to explore new forms of expression.
2. **Collaborate Across Disciplines**
   Working with people from different fields can spark fresh ideas.
   - **Tip:** Join interdisciplinary groups or attend industry events to network with diverse professionals.
3. **Participate in Hackathons or Idea Challenges**
   Events that encourage rapid brainstorming and problem-solving can help you hone your innovative skills.

- **Example:** Look for hackathons hosted by universities or tech hubs in the UK.
4. **Visit Innovation Hotspots**
   Explore places known for fostering creativity, such as London's Design Museum, Manchester's MediaCityUK, or the Science Museum in Birmingham.

Action Steps to Cultivate Creativity and Innovation

1. **Schedule Creative Time**
   Dedicate a specific time each week to brainstorming or exploring new ideas.
2. **Learn Something New**
   Take a course, read a book, or attend a workshop on a topic outside your expertise.
3. **Experiment Without Fear**
   Try a new approach or idea, even if you're unsure of the outcome.
4. **Seek Feedback**
   Share your ideas with trusted friends or colleagues and use their input to refine your approach.

Conclusion: Creativity and Innovation Drive Progress

Creativity and innovation are the forces that propel you forward, helping you solve problems, seize opportunities, and stay ahead in a competitive world. By cultivating a curious mindset, embracing new challenges, and turning ideas into action, you can unlock your potential and create lasting impact.

As you continue your journey to think and act like a winner, remember creativity isn't a gift—it's a skill you can develop. Start small, stay curious, and trust the power of your imagination.

In the next chapter, we'll explore how winners develop leadership qualities to inspire and empower others. But for now, reflect on this: What's one way you can think more creatively or innovate in your work or personal life today?

Great ideas start with bold thinking—begin yours now.

Chapter 26: Leadership – Inspiring and Empowering Others

Leadership isn't about titles or authority—it's about inspiring others, building trust, and creating an environment where people can thrive. Winners understand that effective leadership requires empathy, vision, and the ability to empower those around them. Whether you're leading a team, guiding your family, or simply influencing your community, the principles of leadership apply in every area of life.

In the UK, where collaboration and community values are deeply rooted, leadership often means fostering inclusivity and encouraging diverse voices. From the boardrooms of London to grassroots movements in small towns, effective leaders bring people together to achieve common goals. This chapter explores how winners develop leadership qualities that inspire and empower others.

Why Leadership Matters

"A leader is one who knows the way, goes the way, and shows the way." – John C. Maxwell

Leadership isn't just about getting results—it's about how you achieve them. Great leaders inspire trust, build strong relationships, and create a culture of growth and innovation. They lead by example, showing others what's possible and motivating them to reach their full potential.

Ask yourself: Are you leading by example? Are you inspiring those around you to be their best? Leadership is a skill you can develop by focusing on key principles and practices.

The Core Qualities of Effective Leadership

1. **Vision**
   Great leaders have a clear sense of purpose and direction.
   - **Example:** A school headteacher in the UK might set a vision for improved student outcomes and rally staff, parents, and students to achieve it.
2. **Empathy**
   Understanding others' perspectives fosters trust and collaboration.
   - **Example:** A team leader who listens to their employees' concerns and adapts policies to support work-life balance builds loyalty and morale.

3. **Resilience**
   Leaders remain calm and focused under pressure, guiding others through challenges.
   - **Example:** During the pandemic, many UK business leaders demonstrated resilience by pivoting to new strategies and supporting their teams.
4. **Communication**
   Clear, transparent communication is essential for effective leadership.
   - **Tip:** Use simple, direct language to ensure your message resonates with your audience.
5. **Adaptability**
   Leaders embrace change and encourage others to do the same.
   - **Example:** A manager who adopts flexible working practices empowers their team to succeed in a rapidly changing world.

How Winners Lead by Example

1. **Take Responsibility**
   Leaders own their decisions and actions, whether they succeed or fail.

- **Example:** If a project misses its target, a leader focuses on solutions rather than assigning blame.
2. **Demonstrate Integrity**
Consistency between words and actions builds trust.
    - **Tip:** Honour commitments, admit mistakes, and treat others with respect.
3. **Invest in Others' Growth**
Winners prioritise mentoring and supporting others to achieve their goals.
    - **Example:** Offering career development opportunities, such as training or coaching, inspires loyalty and growth.
4. **Celebrate Success**
Recognising achievements motivates individuals and strengthens team morale.
    - **Tip:** Acknowledge efforts publicly, whether it's through a team meeting, email, or celebratory event.

Leadership in the UK: Cultural Insights

1. **Collaborative Leadership**
UK leaders often emphasise teamwork and inclusivity, fostering a sense of shared purpose.

- **Example:** Football managers like Gareth Southgate have been praised for their ability to unite and motivate their teams, creating an environment of mutual respect.
2. **Community-Focused Leadership**
Grassroots initiatives and local organisations highlight the importance of leadership within communities.
   - **Example:** Local councillors and charity leaders often inspire their communities by addressing pressing issues and advocating for change.
3. **Adapting to Change**
UK businesses and organisations have demonstrated adaptability in response to challenges like Brexit and the pandemic, showing the importance of flexible leadership.

How to Empower Others Through Leadership

1. **Delegate Effectively**
Empowering others to take ownership of tasks builds trust and develops their skills.
   - **Example:** Assigning team members to lead specific projects allows them to gain experience and confidence.

2. **Encourage Collaboration**
   Foster an environment where diverse voices are valued and ideas are shared.
   - **Tip:** Use team-building activities to strengthen relationships and promote open communication.
3. **Provide Constructive Feedback**
   Feedback should focus on growth and improvement, not criticism.
   - **Example:** Highlight strengths while offering actionable suggestions for development.
4. **Lead with Positivity**
   A positive attitude inspires others to stay motivated and resilient.
   - **Tip:** During challenges, focus on solutions and opportunities rather than dwelling on problems.

Case Study: Southgate – Leadership Approach

Gareth Southgate's leadership journey shows that true leadership isn't about authority—it's about inspiring others, building trust, and creating an environment where people can excel. His story underscores the principles explored in this chapter: vision, empathy, resilience, communication, and adaptability.

By leading with purpose and heart, Southgate not only transformed a football team but also inspired a nation.

Overcoming Leadership Challenges

1. **Dealing with Resistance**
   Not everyone will agree with your vision or approach.
   - **Solution:** Listen to concerns, address them with empathy, and explain the rationale behind your decisions.
2. **Balancing Authority and Approachability**
   Leaders must maintain authority while remaining accessible.
   - **Solution:** Set clear boundaries while fostering open communication and trust.
3. **Managing Stress**
   Leadership responsibilities can be overwhelming.
   - **Solution:** Practise self-care and delegate tasks to avoid burnout.

Practical Steps to Develop Leadership Skills in the UK

1. **Seek Mentorship**
   Learn from experienced leaders in your field.
   - **Example:** Join professional organisations like the Institute of Leadership & Management to connect with mentors.
2. **Attend Leadership Workshops**
   Many UK-based institutions offer courses on leadership development.
   - **Tip:** Look for workshops at universities, business schools, or online platforms like FutureLearn.
3. **Volunteer for Leadership Roles**
   Take on leadership responsibilities in community projects, schools, or local charities.
   - **Example:** Chairing a PTA meeting or leading a fundraising campaign can hone your skills.
4. **Read and Learn**
   Explore books, articles, and podcasts on leadership to gain insights and inspiration.
   - **Recommendation:** Start with Simon Sinek's *Start with Why* or Brené Brown's *Dare to Lead*.

Action Steps to Start Leading Today

1. **Define Your Leadership Style**
   Reflect on your strengths, values, and areas for growth as a leader.
2. **Set a Leadership Goal**
   Identify one way you can inspire or empower others this week, whether at work or in your community.
3. **Practice Empathy**
   Make an effort to understand the needs and perspectives of those you lead.
4. **Celebrate Others' Successes**
   Take a moment to acknowledge someone's achievements and show your appreciation.

Conclusion: Leadership is About Empowering Others

Great leaders don't just achieve their own goals — they inspire and empower others to achieve theirs. By cultivating qualities like empathy, resilience, and vision, you can create a positive impact in your workplace, community, and beyond. Leadership isn't about perfection—it's about growth, connection, and the courage to guide others toward a brighter future.

As you continue your journey to think and act like a winner, remember leadership is a responsibility and a privilege. Start small, stay consistent, and lead with purpose.

In the next chapter, we'll explore how achieving harmony amid ambition leads to fulfilment. But for now, reflect on this: What's one action you can take today to inspire or empower someone in your life?

Leadership begins with action—take yours now.

Chapter 27: Balance and Fulfilment – Achieving Harmony Amid Ambition

Pursuing success is rewarding, but it's not the sole ingredient for a fulfilling life. True winners understand the importance of balance—between work and play, ambition and rest, external achievements and inner well-being. They prioritise living a life that not only reaches goals but also feels meaningful and joyful along the way.

In the UK, where long working hours and the "always on" culture can be overwhelming, finding balance is especially vital. This chapter explores how winners maintain harmony in their lives, ensuring that their pursuit of success doesn't come at the expense of happiness or health.

Why Balance and Fulfilment Matter

"Success is not the key to happiness. Happiness is the key to success." – Albert Schweitzer

Balance helps you sustain energy, maintain mental clarity, and nurture relationships. Without it, even the greatest achievements can feel empty. Fulfilment comes from aligning your actions with your values, ensuring that you're thriving in every area of life—not just one.

Ask yourself: Are you living a life of balance, or are you overcommitting to one area while neglecting others? Achieving harmony requires intentional choices and consistent effort.

The Pillars of Balance and Fulfilment

1. **Physical Well-Being**
   Your health is the foundation of everything you do. Prioritising fitness, sleep, and nutrition gives you the energy to pursue your goals.
   - **Example:** Make time for regular exercise, such as cycling through the countryside or attending a local yoga class.
2. **Mental and Emotional Health**
   Caring for your mind and emotions helps you navigate stress and maintain focus.
   - **Tip:** Practise mindfulness, journaling, or therapy to manage your mental health.
3. **Meaningful Relationships**
   Connections with family, friends, and colleagues enrich your life and provide support during challenges.
   - **Example:** Dedicate time each week to catching up with loved ones, whether over a meal or a phone call.

4. **Personal Growth**
   Fulfilment comes from continuous learning and self-discovery.
   - **Example:** Explore a new hobby, take a course, or set aside time for self-reflection.
5. **Purposeful Work**
   Aligning your career with your values ensures that your professional life feels meaningful.
   - **Tip:** Focus on the impact your work has on others, whether you're in a leadership role or a team member.

How Winners Cultivate Balance and Fulfilment

1. **Set Boundaries**
   Winners know when to say "no" to avoid overcommitting and burning out.
   - **Example:** Turn off work emails after hours to protect your personal time.
2. **Prioritise Quality Over Quantity**
   Focus on meaningful activities that align with your values, rather than trying to do it all.
   - **Tip:** Instead of attending every social event, prioritise the ones that matter most to you.

3. **Create Daily Rituals**
   Small, intentional habits create a sense of balance and stability.
   - **Example:** Start your day with a quiet cup of tea or an early morning walk to centre yourself before work.
4. **Celebrate Achievements**
   Recognising your progress fosters gratitude and fulfilment.
   - **Tip:** Treat yourself to a favourite activity or small indulgence when you reach a milestone.

The Challenges of Achieving Balance in the UK

1. **Work Pressure**
   The UK has one of the longest average working weeks in Europe, making it difficult to disconnect.
   - **Solution:** Advocate for flexible working arrangements, such as hybrid or remote work, to create more time for personal priorities.

2. **Cost of Living**
   Rising living costs can create financial stress, making balance feel unattainable.
   - **Solution:** Develop a budget that prioritises essentials and savings, while allowing for small luxuries that bring joy.
3. **Cultural Expectations**
   The UK's "work hard, play hard" ethos can lead to overcommitment in both work and social life.
   - **Solution:** Embrace downtime as a productive part of your routine, essential for recharging and maintaining health.

Case Study: Emma Watson – Balance and Advocacy

Emma Watson, known for her acting career and advocacy work, exemplifies balance. Despite a demanding schedule, Watson prioritises personal growth by pursuing education, maintaining close friendships, and advocating for gender equality through her UN work.

Her ability to align her professional ambitions with her personal values demonstrates that balance and fulfilment are achievable, even in high-pressure roles.

Practical Steps to Create Balance and Fulfilment in the UK

1. **Plan Your Week**
   Schedule time for work, exercise, social activities, and rest to ensure all areas of your life are addressed.
   - **Example:** Use a planner or app to block out specific times for different activities, such as a Sunday roast with family or a midweek gym session.
2. **Disconnect Regularly**
   Take breaks from technology to recharge your mind and connect with the present moment.
   - **Tip:** Set a daily screen-free hour or enjoy a weekend walk in a local park without your phone.
3. **Explore the Outdoors**
   The UK's countryside and coastal areas offer countless opportunities to relax and recharge.
   - **Example:** Visit the Lake District, Cornwall's beaches, or Scotland's Highlands for a weekend escape.
4. **Reflect on Your Values**
   Regularly evaluate whether your actions align with what matters most to you.

- **Tip:** Write down your top three priorities and use them as a guide for decision-making.

Action Steps to Achieve Balance Today

1. **Define Your Priorities**
   Write down the areas of your life that matter most—health, relationships, career, or hobbies—and identify one action to nurture each.
2. **Schedule Rest**
   Plan a day or evening off to relax and enjoy a guilt-free break from your responsibilities.
3. **Reassess Commitments**
   Let go of activities or obligations that don't align with your values or contribute to your well-being.
4. **Celebrate the Present**
   Take a moment today to appreciate something you've achieved or enjoyed recently. Gratitude fosters a sense of balance and fulfilment.

Conclusion: Balance is the Key to a Fulfilling Life

Balance and fulfilment are not about perfection—they're about making intentional choices that honour your values, nurture your well-being, and create joy in your daily life. Winners understand that true success isn't just about achieving goals—it's about enjoying the journey.

As you continue your journey to think and act like a winner, remember balance is an ongoing process, not a destination. Take small steps each day to create harmony in your life, and trust that fulfilment will follow.

Harmony begins with intention—make yours today.

Summary of the Book

This book has explored the essential qualities, habits, and mindsets that define winners, providing practical guidance to help you achieve success and fulfilment in your personal and professional life. Each chapter focused on a core principle or practice, offering actionable insights to inspire and empower you on your journey. Below is a recap of the key takeaways from the book:

Key Takeaways

- **Success is a Journey, Not a Destination:** It's about who you become in the process, not just what you achieve.
- **Growth Requires Action:** Small, consistent steps lead to transformative results.
- **Mindset Shapes Your Reality:** Cultivate positivity, resilience, and gratitude to navigate challenges and seize opportunities.
- **Relationships Enrich Success:** Invest in meaningful connections that support and inspire you.
- **Balance Brings Fulfilment:** Prioritise health, relationships, and rest alongside ambition to achieve sustainable success.

Final Reflection

Success is within your reach. By embracing the principles and practices outlined in this book, you can create a life of purpose, achievement, and joy. Start small, stay consistent, and trust in your ability to grow and thrive.

Take action today and remember thinking and acting like a winner begins with the choices you make in each moment. Success is not just about what you do—it's about who you are.

What will your next step be on the path to becoming a winner?

www.ingramcontent.com/pod-product-compliance
Lightning Source LLC
Chambersburg PA
CBHW071635220526
45469CB00002B/627